BI 3467767

D1756217

THE JEWESS OF TOLEDO
THE INNOCENT CHILD

Lope de Vega

PLAYS ONE

THE JEWESS OF TOLEDO
THE INNOCENT CHILD

translated by
Michael Jacobs

OBERON BOOKS
LONDON

First published in 2001 by Oberon Books Ltd.
(incorporating Absolute Classics)
521 Caledonian Road, London N7 9RH
Tel: 020 7607 3637 / Fax: 020 7607 3629

e-mail: oberon.books@btinternet.com

A catalogue record for this book is available from the British
Library.

ISBN: 1 84002 144 6

Cover design: Andrzej Klimowski

Typography: Richard Doust

Printed in Great Britain by Antony Rowe Ltd, Reading.

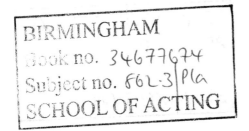

Contents

these translations are dedicated
to Colin Elwood

Introduction

Michael Jacobs

O f all the giants of world drama, Lope de Vega has suffered more than most from the vagaries of reputation. Adored in his life-time more by the theatre-going masses than by the courtly and literary circles whose recognition he craved, Lope is today a playwright whose full theatrical range is known essentially only to a scholarly elite. His fame, so unfairly, has come largely to rest on a tiny fraction of his plays, few of which are regularly performed, even in the Spanish-speaking world. Though he is generally acknowledged as the greatest playwright in the Spanish language, he continues everywhere to be neglected in favour of his contemporary Shakespeare. And yet if the supremacy of Shakespeare's position were to be seriously challenged by anyone, it would surely be by Lope, whose works above those of all other dramatists of this period have a comparable variety of tone and subject-matter, a similarly vast array of characters, and a shared wealth of ambiguities that allows for constant re-interpretation.

Perhaps, as has even been suggested, had the Spanish Armada been victorious, had Protestantism been defeated by the Counter-Reformation, and had circumstances generally been more favourable to Spain than to Britain, Shakespeare might well have been overshadowed by Lope[1]. However, the main hurdle that Lope has faced is surely not history but rather the unrivalled fecundity that led this man whom Cervantes notoriously called the 'monster of nature' to write possibly as many as 1,500 plays, of which at least 350 remain. This frighteningly fast rate of production, though undoubtedly exaggerated by Lope himself, is sufficiently daunting to put off anyone from studying his works, and, understandably, is sometimes thought of as his principle claim to fame.

The general assumption that quantity on this scale is surely incompatible with quality seems confirmed by the relatively

[1] See Jonathan Bate, *The Genius of Shakespeare*, London, 1997

small canon of great plays that has been established since Lope's death. But how reliable is this canon? In looking more widely over Lope's work, it has become increasingly apparent in recent years that the most famous of his plays are not necessarily the best. Indeed, a disproportionately high number of the accepted classics are accessible cloak and dagger works whose popularity has probably been enhanced by the fact that they fulfil stereotypical notions of the Spaniards as an honour-obsessed race. In contrast, among the notable absences from the canon are those plays of his in which religion plays a vital part. Their subject-matter can clearly cause difficulties for non-Catholic audiences. But their neglect over the centuries might be connected as well with the strikingly unconventional structure and frequently bizarre touches characteristic of the most interesting of these works. These very qualities, though disturbing to traditional sensibilities, are, of course, precisely what make these plays so ripe for modern reassessment.

Forgotten plays by major playwrights are usually best forgotten; but this is certainly not the case with Lope, whose works are likely to yield exciting 'discoveries' for many years to come. Some of these revelations will doubtless emerge as more and more of his plays are translated. As well as playing a crucial role in making Lope better known internationally (at present less than a tenth of his output can be read other than in Spanish), the efforts of recent translators have drawn the attention of the Spaniards themselves to a number of dramatic gems that have been scarcely performed, if at all, since the seventeenth century. One such work is *Lo fingido verdadero* (literally 'The Feigning of the Truth'), which, until the 1980's, was largely remembered as the basis for the French writer Jean Rotrou's highly successful play *Le Véritable Saint Genest* (1645). A faithful if rather stilted English translation of 1986[2] had at least the virtue of showing that this devotional drama on the unpromising theme of Saint Genesius's conversion to Christianity had a startlingly modern resonance. Five years

---

[2] Michael D. McGaha, *Acting is Believing, a tragicomedy in three acts by Lope de Vega (c.1607-1608), Trinity University Press, San Antonio, Texas, 1986*

later, when produced at London's Gate Theatre in a free and lively version called the *The Great Pretenders*, the play was revealed as a lost masterpiece on the theme of reality and illusion[3].

The translations that make up this present volume were also attempts to give new theatrical life to two works that had survived into modern times largely as historical curiosities. Little valued by scholars for their dramatic potential, *The Jewess of Toledo* and *The Innocent Child* had once seemed of interest primarily for being Lope's only two, non-Biblical plays to portray the Jews, and for having popularised respectively a renowned thirteenth-century love story and a gruesome tale of the Spanish Inquisition.

The historically questionable story that forms the basis of *The Jewess of Toledo* concerns the love of Spain's great military leader Alfonso VIII for a Jewess whom Lope named Rachel. This is a story that, in Lope's telling, would give rise to numerous later versions, notably a far more celebrated play of the same title by the nineteenth-century Austrian dramatist Grillparzer[4]. Lope's own source was a 1541 edition of the chronicle of Spanish history written in the thirteenth century under the supervision of Alfonso's great grandson, Alfonso the Wise. Though at times Lope followed this account remarkably closely, he took a number of significant historical liberties, including the entire invention of Alfonso's involvement in the Crusades. As one might have expected from a dramatist who clearly loved writing strong female roles, he also departed from recorded history in his depiction of the women in Alfonso's life. He created an early distraction for Alfonso in the form of the independent-minded Costanza, and even has her appearing on a castle's battlements in defiance of historical plausibility. And he transformed Alfonso's submissive English-born wife Leonor into a powerful woman of action by showing that it was she rather than his knights who initiated the plot against Rachel.

[3] Published in David Johnston, *Two Plays by Lope de Vega. The Great Pretenders, The Gentleman from Olmedo*, Absolute Classics, Bath, 1992

[4] Franz Grillparzer, *Die Judin von Toledo*; worked on apparently for over twenty years (1833-1855), and not premiered until 1873, this has been translated into several languages

As for Rachel, Lope tried as far as possible to flesh out the faceless *femme fatale* of legend. Of course, in a Spain under the thumb of the Inquisition and obsessed by the notion of 'purity of blood', there was a limit as to how far he could show a Jew in a kindly light. None the less, artistic instinct in Lope seems to have run counter to what might have been expected of him as a Spaniard and a Catholic. In the interests of a more emotionally engaging and plausible drama, Lope clearly felt that his audience should sympathise to some degree with Rachel's plight. When she is first introduced to us, she expressed feelings that were surely intended to rouse the patriotic feelings of a Spanish audience. She says that the fact of her not being a Christian does not make her any less of a Spaniard, and that she is proud to be from a land so much more conducive to passion and sensuality than the cold northern climes from where Leonor comes. Towards the end of the play, when Leonor displays the passionate depths of her own character, and Rachel is being hunted down as a 'Hebrew witch', Lope still seems keen to ensure that his public perceives the Jewess in human terms. Alfonso's knights are shown as sadistically blood-thirsty, while Rachel is depicted as a victim of her own beauty and susceptibility to love. While Lope's decision to go against the known facts and have her convert suddenly to Christianity on the point of death might seem to us now rather token, it enabled the audiences of his day openly to be touched by her tragic end.

But in assessing this play we would be wrong to dwell too much either on its Jewish aspects or even on its decidedly sketchy treatment of Alfonso's affair with Rachel. The greatness of the work, and the reason perhaps why it has been neglected at the expense of later, more conventional versions of the Rachel legend, is that it was clearly intended as far more than a mere love story. This is made evident both by its full and unwieldy Spanish title (*Las paces de los Reyes, y la judía de Toledo*, or 'The King's Peace Treaties, and The Jewess of Toledo) and by its having a first act that takes place long before Alfonso ever met Rachel. Beginning at a time when Christian Spain is split over the issue of the guardianship of the fatherless ten-year-old Alfonso, the play develops into a complex stories of divided loyalties and internal conflict.

Cervantes, in his *Don Quixote*, commented on the absurdity of having a play in which a king is shown one moment as a boy and the next as a grown man. However, this play's peculiar structure, rather than being a weakness, reveals the sureness and originality of Lope's dramatic instinct. Though each of the acts is set many years apart a remarkable unity is given to the whole by having scenes from the time of Alfonso's childhood being constantly echoed in ones from his maturity. Thus, to give just three examples, Costanza's disarming influence on the child Alfonso prepares us for the way in which Rachel detracts him in later life from the affairs of state; the servant Dominguillo's disloyalty towards his friend and master Lope de Arenas is exactly parallelled in Alfonso's betrayal by his life-long companion Garcerán; and the scene of physical blindness with which the first act closes prefigures the state of metaphorical blindness in which the king finds himself at the end of the second act. This whole structure is in turn reflected in the play's constant allusions to mirrors, as, for instance, when Alfonso's son Enrique is referred to as a mirror being held up before Alfonso to remind the latter how he himself once was. There are even two dramatically innovative moments when Alfonso's thoughts are shown mirrored by Leonor's, thus implying the perfect balance that exists in their relationship, and the shattering consequences of Rachel's intrusion.

Another unifying feature is the setting of Toledo, a town whose associations for Lope's public embody the different spheres on which the play moves. The seat of the Spanish Court during Alfonso's time, as well as the home of the country's largest community of Jews, it lived on after the 16th century as the spiritual capital of Spain, and remains to this day a bastion of the Spanish church and army. The main base from which the Christian 'reconquest' of Spain was undertaken, Toledo has also been the scene of some of the more unattractive moments in Spanish history. Among these was the storming in 1405 of the synagogue of Santa María la Blanca, an action that brought to an end centuries of relatively harmonious coexistence between Jews and Christians, and initiated some of the worst pogroms before the twentieth century.

Appropriately, in view of the concern shown by Lope's knights in the antiquity of their Christian lineage, it was also in Toledo that a proposal was made in 1547 to allow into the Church only those Christians without any traces of Moorish or Jewish blood.

Yet belying this urban symbol of repression, so eloquently evoked by the thorn-like spikes crowning the town's towering cathedral, is a place that once enjoyed a sensual reputation. The women of Toledo were thought of as the most beautiful in the country, in particular its Jewesses, in whom was dangerously expressed all the guilt-free sexuality and sybaritic languor traditionally linked with Muslim Spain. Moreover, the banks of the Tagus, where Alfonso first sets eyes on the naked Rachel, and where their affair is carried out, were a well known pleasure retreat which attracted by the late sixteenth century a high proportion of the town's prostitutes.

This outlying erotic domain, so powerfully contrasted in Lope's play with the world of courtly pomp and church ceremonial centred on the town above, contains as well some of the elements that contribute to Toledo's continuing fame as a place of magic and the occult. Here, in the outskirts of Toledo, were situated two of Spain's most potent mythical sites, both of which are referred to by Lope. One of these, identified in his day by some overgrown riverside ruins, was the summer palace of the Moorish princess Galiana, who seduced the young Charlemagne by ensnaring him with her magical powers. The other was the 'secret chamber' that none of Spain's kings was allowed to enter, the penalty for doing so being the conquest of their country by the Moors. Lope's king, in keeping with the real Alfonso's known action in beautifying the Tagus's banks, restores Galiana's ruined palace as a home for Rachel, and pursues here an affair whose consequences are likened to the fatal ones arising out of the penetration of the 'secret chamber' by the Visigothic king Roderick. Significantly, as Alfonso goes outside Toledo's walls and descends down to the river, he is greeted by supernatural visions and a terrifying thunderstorm that leaves the upper town untouched.

The Jewess of Toledo, as with so much of Lope de Vega's drama, is deeply revealing of what we know about the playwright's own life and personality. Toledo itself seems to have held an important place in his heart; and though he wrote the play in Madrid he must have thought back during the writing of it to a characteristically intensive period when he was living in the town with both his wife Juana de Guardo and his mistress Micaela de Luján, and managing to have children almost simultaneously with both of them. More importantly, the play, in moving freely between the worlds of the spirit and the senses, reflects the constant alternation in Lope's character between erotic obsessions and bouts of religiosity. Appropriately, in the years immediately preceding the writing of this work, Lope had taken up the priesthood and then fallen passionately in love (at the age of fifty-three) with the beautiful Marta de Nevares, a young married woman who was to have his last child.

The sexual aspects of Lope's life and work are more accessible than the religious ones, at least for a modern British audience. The church scene dénouement of *The Jewess of Toledo*, with its interceding miraculous image of the Virgin, and the convenient way in which Alfonso is suddenly able to overcome his seven-year obsession with Rachel, is certainly the part of the play most difficult for us now to accept. Despite this, however, when the play was put on under the most stressful conditions at London's Bridewell Theatre in 1997, the work had an impact far greater than anyone involved in the production had imagined. After attracting initially small and predominantly Jewish audiences, it soon drew a much wider response, and ended up playing to packed houses and being featured on the main Spanish news programmes. For all its apparent structural waywardness and Catholic preoccupations the central and universal theme of the struggle between duty and erotic passion had emerged with visceral force.

Sadly, a similar opportunity to risk a full-scale production of a strange and neglected work is unlikely to materialise in

[5] *El niño inocente de la Guardia*

13

the case of *The Innocent Child* [5]. This tale of a group of Jews using an eleven-year-old Christian to recreate Christ's passion is one of the most shocking and disturbing of Lope's plays. The translation that appears here was commissioned in 1998 by Shakespeare's Globe as one of a number of staged readings to accompany a production of *The Merchant of Venice*. The musicians who were going to take part walked out at the last moment, complaining not simply of what they believed to be the play's unrelieved anti-Semitism but also of the undertones of sadism and even paedophilia. In the end most of those who participated in and witnessed the event were more carried away by the exciting pace and theatricality of the work than by any moral scruples. None the less it was with a certain trepidation that I stepped out afterwards on to the stage to argue that what might seem superficially a crude piece of Catholic propaganda was a deeply ambivalent and possibly subversive work.

The Innocent Child, which was probably written only a few years before the expulsion in 1610 of all of Spain's remaining Moriscos or citizens of Moorish blood, reflects the hysteria about racial origins that had taken root after the founding of the Spanish Inquisition in 1481. The Inquisition was established with the almost exclusive aim of detecting and punishing the secret Jewish practices of Spain's 'conversos' or 'New Christians'; soon it had to deal as well with the thousands of 'false converts' created by the enforced conversion of Spain's Muslims after 1499. A climate of mounting fear and suspicion resulted, with accusations made out of personal spite, properties confiscated on the slightest pretence, and – as Lope shows us in his play – neighbours spying upon neighbours. In such a racially mixed country as Spain, the scope for potentially damaging racial slurs was limitless. Both the notorious inquisitor Torquemada and Isabella's husband Ferdinand (who are holding a meeting on the Jewish 'heresy' when *The Innocent Child* begins) were themselves 'impure', the former having been a converso and the latter having had a Jewish mother. Interestingly, though Lope himself was unquestionably an 'Old Christian', evidence suggests that he was obliged to clear his name on account of aspersions made against him on the basis of his father having practised a trade associated with the Jews.

It is against this background that the ghastly true tale on which Lope based his play should be seen. The historical 'facts' concern a Jewish convert to Christianity called Benito García, who, in 1490, was found returning from a pilgrimage to Santiago de Compostela with a consecrated host in his knapsack. He was handed over immediately to the Inquisition. After days of torture that included having wires pulled tightly around his limbs and water poured down his throat, Benito confessed to belonging to a group of Jewish and converso conspirators from the village of la Guardia near Toledo. Those whom he named were subsequently rounded up and tortured themselves, after which a story emerged involving the crucifying of a young Christian child in a cave, and a plan to mingle his blood with the consecrated host in Benito's possession. Accusations of defiling the host and using a child to recreate Christ's Passion and Crucifixion have been made against Jews throughout history, and helped greatly to justify the most repressive measures on the part of the authorities: the story of what supposedly happened at La Guardia seems to have influenced the decision of Ferdinand and Isabella to expel the Jews from Spain in 1492.

None of the confessions extracted in the La Guardia case tallied, no boy's body was ever found, and all the original documentation mysteriously disappeared. This lack of hard facts proved enormously useful in fostering in sixteenth and seventeenth-century Spain the growing cult of the Boy of La Guardia: the absence of a body was taken as evidence that the boy's earthly remains were brought straight to heaven, and even the conflicting stories about whether the boy was called Juan or Cristobal were given a divine explanation. The house of one of the conspirators was pulled down to make way for a church, and the cave was turned into a shrine; by the early seventeenth century the Chapter of Toledo was petitioning for the child's sanctification.

Lope's presumed anti-Semitic motives in glorifying a dubious cult which even the Vatican paid little heed to would seem at first difficult to dispute, especially given the playwright's own close links with the Inquisition. The nephew of an inquisitor still remembered in Seville by the phrase 'as bloody as Carpio', Lope became himself an officer of the Inquisition in 1608, and assisted in the tribunal of an *Auto da Fe* twenty years later. However, nothing about Lope is entirely straightforward, and not even the fact that he was an active supporter of the Inquisition precludes the possibility that he was also one of this institution's most devious critics.

In studying Lope one is not only dealing with a playwright whose works were conditioned more by instinct and a sense of humanity than by any rigid doctrine. One is also struggling to understand one of the most labyrinthine personalities in the history of literature. The eventfulness of Lope's life, and the mass of documentation at one's disposal make him in many ways a biographer's dream; but the perplexingly contradictory nature of this material explain perhaps why no truly satisfactory biography on him has appeared. Such is the wealth of interpretations that his life and work encourage, and such is the quantity of material available to back up even the most far-flung theories, that articles can be written, say, on Lope's views on astrology that could equally prove or disprove his interest in the subject.

How wrong one can in fact be about Lope is shown by the way he managed almost to have gone down in history as a saintly and even divine figure. Already the subject in his lifetime of an anonymous prayer in which God's name was blasphemously replaced by his, he found himself constantly approached in the streets of Madrid by those seeking his blessing or wishing to touch his cloak. This reputation was later consolidated by his contemporary biographer Pérez de Montalbán, whose idealised account of Lope's life went completely unchallenged until the late nineteenth century. From that time onwards facts emerged showing that this pillar of the Catholic Church was a sinner on a scale that even Graham Greene in his more indulgent moments could not have conceived.

Even the powerful simplicity of so much of his art can be deceptive. *The Innocent Child*, though based on a popular and unsophisticated religious tale, contains in fact two plays of radically different tone. On the one hand we find a simple devotional play that pits the forces of goodness and light against those of darkness and evil, and which mitigates the gruesome horrors of the child's martyrdom with the joys that await him in paradise. On the other hand there is play full of black humour, cynical observation, and reversals of expectation. Remarkably, the Christians are shown at times to be as devious and money-grasping as the Jews, while the latter are presented initially as so sympathetic as to be allowed, so unusually for Golden Age Spain, a lyrical lament about the consequences of Isabella's act of expulsion. This lament, with its moving description of the Jews leaving their homes, curiously recalls the scenes of departing moriscos as recorded in 1610 by one Father Aznar Cardona, who perceived the refugees as 'tired, in pain, lost, exhausted, sad, confused, ashamed, angry, crestfallen, irritated, bored, thirsty and hungry'.

Perhaps the most significant clue as to the possible underlying intentions of *The Innocent Child* can be found in the changes made by Lope to the chronology of events. In having his Jewish and converso conspirators commit their crimes immediately after rather than before the expulsion order of 1492, and in having the Inquisition founded at the same time as this order was issued, Lope is not simply giving a greater dramatic power to the story: he is also suggesting, however unwittingly, that the transformation of the Jews from reasonable beings into murderous psychopaths was a direct result of these cruel developments in Spanish history. Such a reading of the play can easily be condemned as that of a twenty-first-century liberal; but surely part of the genius of Lope lies in the different meanings his works can have to successive generations. By looking at *The Innocent Child* with an open mind, unprejudiced by its subject-matter, the work can be viewed as a rivetting and sometimes blackly farcical comment on the self-perpetuating nature of intolerance and brutality.

Inevitably, with such a finely nuanced playwright as Lope, an especially large burden falls upon the translator. It is essential to try and do justice to the plays' abundance of puns, ironies, and double meanings, and also to capture the relentless shifts of tone that exist not just from one scene to the next but within each scene itself. Lyricism and rhetoric give way suddenly to coarseness and astonishing naturalism, and – in a way that seems startlingly modern – moments of solemnity and tragedy are punctuated by ones of farce and absurdity. Thus, Leonor's fervent praying in church in the closing scene of *The Jewess of Toledo* is interrupted by the arrival of Garcerán asking her to lower her voice; and the climactic plunging of the knife in *The Innocent Child* is followed by a request to 'pass the salt'.

This remarkable variety of mood is enhanced in the original Spanish by Lope's characteristic use of several different verse forms. To try and find English equivalents for these would be a dry and academic exercise, while rendering the whole in blank or rhyming verse would risk both monotony and a loss of the texts' exciting immediacy. These considerations, together with the fact that Lope's predominantly octosyllabic verse can sound almost indistinguishable from prose in recitation, has led me to opt for what are essentially prose translations. While I have turned to verse for some of the more obvious set-pieces in *The Jewess of Toledo*, I have generally aimed to match Lope's more lyrical moments with a suitably sonorous prose; elsewhere I have tried to achieve a fluently colloquial style which, I hope, is not too glaringly modern. Ultimately, I do not believe in too hard and fast an approach to the translation of Lope's plays, and indeed follow the empirical line advocated by Lope himself in his *The New Art of Making Plays in This Age*. What is important is that the works are entertaining, performable, and freed from the tyrannies of scholars.

Michael Jacobs
London, 2001

THE JEWESS OF TOLEDO

Characters

DON ESTEBAN ILLÁN
COUNT MANRIQUE
ELVIRA, his wife
LOPE DE ARENAS
COSTANZA, his wife
DOMINGUILLO, a jester
LISEÑO, a servant
FERNAN RUÍZ DE CASTRO
PEDRO DÍEZ
KING ALFONSO VIII
DON NUÑO
QUEEN LEONOR
GARCERÁN MANRIQUE, son of Count Manrique
DON ILLÁN, son of Don Esteban Illan
CLARA, Leonor's Lady-in-Waiting
DON BLASCO DE GUZMÁN, governor of Toledo
BELTRÁN THE RED
MENDOZA, a servant

RACHEL, a Jewess
DAVID, her father
SIBILA, her sister
LEVI, her brother

BELARDO, a gardener
FILENO, a gardener
BARBER
SOLDIERS

This translation of *The Jewess of Toledo* was first performed by Stranger's Gallery at the Bridewell Theatre, London, on 6 February 1997, with the following cast:

DON ESTEBAN/BELTRÁN, Roger Barclay

COUNT MANRIQUE/DAVID, Alistair Maydon

ELVIRA/CLARA, Amy Oliver

LOPE DE ARENAS/BELARDO, David Delve

COSTANZA, Rosalind Croft

DOMINGUILLO/ILLÁN, David Birrell

LISEÑO/LEVI, Iain Patterson

FERNÁN/FILENO, Paul Rattee

PEDRO DIEZ/MENDOZA, Peter Elliot

ALFONSO (as child), Ben Hayward/Jonathan Richards/ Matthew Evans

ALFONSO (as adult), Simon Chadwick

NUÑO, Roy Ward

LEONOR, Charlotte Christie

GARCERÁN MANRIQUE (as child), William Ross-Foulser/James Rattee

GARCERÁN (as adult), Russell Layton

BLASCO, Roy Ward

RACHEL, Michelle Gomez

SIBILA, Carol Kentish

BARBER, SOLDIERS, The Company

Director/Producer, Colin Ellwood

Designer, Bridget Kimak

Music, The Dufay Collective

Lighting, Nick Peel

Sound, Crispian Covell

Production Manager, Stephen Ward

Stage Manager, Emily Jones

ACT ONE

DON ESTEBAN ILLÁN and COUNT MANRIQUE are standing on the tower of the Toledan church of San Roman.

COUNT: Toledo for Alfonso, rightful King
   of Castile! Toledo for Alfonso,
   son of King Sancho the Fair,
   grandson of the Spanish Emperor!
DON ESTEBAN: Toledo for Alfonso, Castillians,
   not for Ferdinand of Leon, his uncle!
   Alfonso's your king! Long live Alfonso!
   (*Enter below FERNÁN RUIZ and LOPE DE ARENAS,
   together with a large crowd of soldiers with unsheathed swords.*)
FERNÁN: Who's stirring up the city, soldiers?
   What's this I hear about long live Alfonso?
   Don't you know that Toledo's in the protection
   of Ferdinand of Leon, and that I'm guarding
   its citadel for him, and that its walls
   won't be given up to Castile until Alfonso's
   reached the age of fifteen, as his father had
   decreed? Who's behind all this shouting?
COUNT: Fernán Ruíz, even though Ferdinand is
   claiming Toledo's taxes, and is unfairly
   calling himself its lord, you know
   as well as I do that Alfonso is the rightful king;
   you know how Ferdinand has always set his eyes on
   the kingdom, and that the boy is only alive
   thanks to the loyalty of the knights of
   Ávila, who have looked after him since birth.
   Toledo wants now to surrender to its king; let
   the King, at long last, enjoy Toledo.
FERNÁN: But as the city is protected by Ferdinand,
   how can a mere child have any right to its taxes?
DON ESTEBAN: The written agreement was clear:
   if Alfonso enters Toledo,
   the citizens are obliged to obey him.

23

LOPE: That's true, Esteban;
    but you can't just wander into the city like that.
    And why wage your campaign from that tower?
    I admit it's high, but it's hardly strong.
DON ESTEBAN: If Alfonso himself was now in Toledo,
    and I could make him appear in front of you,
    you would surely have no other choice but to obey him?
FERNÁN: But that's ridiculous, how
    could a little boy get through these defences?
    (*ALFONSO, the Child King appears high up in the tower.*)
DON ESTEBAN: Castillians, isn't this Alfonso?
    Isn't this your king?
FERNÁN: Heavens! I can't believe what I'm seeing!
DON ESTEBAN: For those of you who are pure Spaniards,
    here is your king, Alfonso.
COUNT: Speak, sire; tell them all who you are.
ALFONSO: Most noble Castillians,
    I am the King of Castille
    Aren't I lucky to have
    such good guardians as these?
    It is to them that I owe
    the life that my scheming uncle has
    tried so often to take away.
    Manrique has placed me on the walls of
    Toledo and given me a loyal,
    true and noble heart.
    This is Esteban Illán,
    who, in my landless state,
    has granted me as citadel
    the tower of San Roman.
    Here I am. If I'm not welcome
    fight me; for I can tell you now
    that I'll be well defended.
    Come on, turn your swords
    against your king; come up and get me!
FERNÁN: My lord, the King, listen.
ALFONSO: Go on then, speak!
FERNÁN: Our swords will stay where they are,
    no Castillian will ever raise one against you;

God, the all powerful, would never allow it.
The city that was once mine
is all yours; however, I cannot
serve on you here.
You know what my position is:
the issue of your upbringing
has turned the Laras against the Castros;
the sword alone can resolve our differences.
The Count is well aware of this.

COUNT: I am indeed.
I've never wavered in my loyalty.

FERNÁN: Yes, but that's a lesson you learnt from me.

COUNT: I'll always hunt you down.

FERNÁN: I'll be waiting for you, Manrique.

(*Exit everyone at the bottom of the tower, except LOPE.*)

LOPE: Even though Toledo is now prepared
to hand over her keys to Alfonso
I'm not obliged to give up Zurita castle
until the King is fifteen years old,
whether he comes here earlier or not.

COUNT: Lope, follow the example of the nobility.

LOPE: If this is contrary to the will of the King,
his father, then why should I give up
what you can so easily take away?
To hold on to it is the only choice I have.
How do I know that one of you won't snatch the throne
himself,
no sooner have you the power in your hands?

COUNT: I can hardly believe that
there could be such a man among us;
someone who has protected the King
from his uncle's fury,
who has helped and defended him
and constantly risked his own life,
from the time the King was just a baby;
how could such a person be then blinded by ambition
to stoop so low?

ALFONSO: Lope de Arenas…

LOPE: Sire…

ALFONSO: Why don't you give me your castle?
    Don't you know I'm the King?
DON ESTEBAN: What wonderful directness!
LOPE: The person who entrusted it to me
    was loyal to your father.
ALFONSO: Is that how you reply to a king?
LOPE: If you agree your father was a just man, yes.
    I can only repeat, sire, that the castle
    cannot be yours until you are fifteen.
ALFONSO: Isn't the loyalty of my people good enough for
                       you?
LOPE: I'm afraid it is not.
ALFONSO: In that case I'll have myself crowned in Toledo,
    and then take my castle by force.
LOPE: As you wish, sire;
    go ahead and try and capture it,
    I cannot give it to you.
    (*Exit.*)
ALFONSO: Well, what do you think of him?
COUNT: It would seem that by his good intentions
    he wishes only to betray you
    not to defend you.
    Let's crown you immediately
    and then draw our swords.
ALFONSO: I can't wait to draw mine,
    if only I had one.
    Please, count, can't you knight me now
    and give me my sword.
    Then you'll see me putting a stop
    to my uncle's tyranny.
COUNT: We'll give you first the crown,
    and then the sword of knighthood.
    Then forward to Zurita!
    I see you have the makings of a brave and noble leader,
    we'll soon have to call you Alfonso the Good.
ALFONSO: Count, only God is GOOD.
    (*The COUNT is left on his own with DON ESTEBAN.*)
DON ESTEBAN: Aren't you amazed by this precocious lad,
    who seems destined in his land

to be remembered as a Caesar in war,
and a Numa Pompilius in peace?
(*Exit both. Enter COSTANZA and DOMINQUILLO.*)

COSTANZA: (*Constance.*) Lope's taking his time in Toledo;
something serious must be going on.

DOMINGUILLO: I can't imagine, my lady,
that there's anything sinister in his delay
We know that Alfonso's up-in-arms and wants his crown,
but Fernán Ruíz, a good Castillian,
holds Toledo for Ferdinand of Leon.
The gates are strongly guarded
by his armed supporters.

COSTANZA: I have a faithful heart
and past events have taught me
to worry about the present.

DOMINGUILLO: To love is to worry –
that's what love's all about.

COSTANZA: The supporters of Alfonso
seem to cause nothing but trouble.
Most Castillians think my husband's right
in sticking to the father's will.

DOMINGUILLO: My lady, I feel the same,
to support Alfonso is madness.
Why should the boy receive the taxes
that he's come to collect
if he's still too young
to know what to do with them?
It's much better that they be kept for him
until he's old enough to rule.
Your love surprises me, I have to say:
there was I, wrongly thinking that
your worries for your husband's lateness
were all to do with jealousy of Toledo's women.
Instead I see you frightened by Alfonso's knights.

COSTANZA: If you can only love someone
by being suspicious and jealous,
then surely it's much better for a woman
to love her husband by worrying about his life.
(*Enter a SERVANT.*)

SERVANT: My master's at the castle gate.

COSTANZA: Take this ring to him, Liseño,
    tell him how relieved I am he's safe and sound.
    He is all right, isn't he?

SERVANT: In fighting form, and ready to defend this fortress.

COSTANZA: Against whom?

SERVANT: The King.

COSTANZA: What's forced him into this?

SERVANT: He says he gave his word to Alfonso's father,
    he's no other choice but to respect the will.

COSTANZA: Give the fortress straight to the King,
    that's what I'd do.
    You can always protest later.

DOMINGUILLO: What? Why should he give in to the
                                King's demands
    when he's only following the letter of the law?

COSTANZA: Domingo, you don't argue with God,
    and you don't with the King either.
    I must talk to him immediately.
    (*Exit.*)

DOMINGUILLO: Tell me.
    What the hell's going on in Toledo?

SERVANT: Nothing too dramatic so far.
    All that's happened is that Don Esteban Illán
    has smuggled the King into the city
    and made a base in the tower of San Román.

DOMINGUILLO: But if Alfonso's in Toledo,
    then the city's his
    and all who oppose him are lost:
    only the toughest will survive.

SERVANT: Nonsense, there are many other fortresses;
    and this is the strongest of them all.

DOMINGUILLO: You certainly are loyal to our master.
    God be with you!

SERVANT: I'm going to help him dismount.
    (*Exit.*)

DOMINGUILLO: At the end of the day,
    I've got to find my daily bread.

If I can give the King the fortress
then I'll certainly be well rewarded;
but how can I even say such a thing
when I owe everything to Don Lope de Arenas –
the very life I lead,
my upbringing, my present well-being?
I know why: it's because
I see myself losing all that I possess.
What's over is over,
life's too short to think
too much about the past,
the future's all that matters.
What's going to be best for me?
That's what I've got to ask.
And, if I'm being honest,
it's my position of trust
that'll serve my interests best.
When my deviousness is out,
I know too well what all of Spain will say:
he was a traitor to his master
but a saviour to his king.
(*Exit and enter the King's Guard followed by the COUNT,
DON ESTEBAN, ELVIRA wife of the COUNT and the
Child King himself.*)

COUNT: Glorious Alfonso, Sancho's one and only heir,
from the greatest of soldiers you have nothing to fear;
your years of darkness are now banished by the light.
You have come here today to be dubbed a knight.
As rightful heir to that invincible, incomparable lord,
listen carefully to your duties on being handed the sword.
The law of God, Alfonso, the Holy Faith itself you must
defend
and make Her Glory force the knees of trembling Moors
to bend.
To the land of al-Andalus you must deliver such a blow
that the pure waters of our Tagus with its blood will flow.
Protect your country and your kingdom and they'll be
yours,

29

and be sure to emulate your grandfather in issuing just laws.
Remember, finally, that even a phoenix is of woman born.
To the defence of women's rights may your sword be sworn.
Will you swear to all this?

ALFONSO: Manrique, I hope that with your generous help
I shall protect the faith and my beloved homeland.

COUNT: In Castille, the custom for knighting our men
is to have them unveil
a statue of James the apostle
which was rescued from the Moors.
This image has such strange powers that
it can not only knight you, but it can
also bring you luck for the rest of your life.

ALFONSO: Manrique, can an actual statue take part in a
ceremony?

COUNT: If it's this one sire, it can;
this statue is so ingeniously made
that anyone who kneels before it
is touched by its sword.

ALFONSO: Let me pray to the Apostle
to be always victorious in battle

COUNT: Climb up to the altar;
he will be able to hear you better.
(*An armed, equestrian statue of St James, with a golden sword
in one of his hands, is revealed above the steps and the altar.*)

ALFONSO: Saint James, cousin of Christ Our Lord,
celestial knight with the shining sword
who has come to Spain in her times of need,
and led us to glory on your dark black steed.

I'm asking you now to guard the tender life
of a little boy brought up on war and strife,
a careworn king who was already old at birth,
who has never known a father, nor any mirth.

I put myself gladly in your loving care –
with you as a father I have nothing to fear.
If you lend me your strong, paternal hand,
I know I'll be safe from my uncle Ferdinand.

Please knight me now with your sharp steel,
and I'll even bring the blackest Moor to heel.
I'll colour this sword such a violent red
that it'll incite all Spaniards who are nobly bred.

'For God and St James!' will be our battle cry,
We'll shout this out and be prepared to die
until our fair Castille is at peace once more,
and the whole of Spain united under Christian law.
(*To the accompaniment of music the statue dubs and blesses
him. He then walks back down the steps.*)

DON ESTEBAN: Now that the King is knighted,
    our custom here is for a woman
    to help him on with his spurs.

COUNT: Esteban, my wife Elvira has taken upon
    herself this noble duty.
    Be seated, sire.

ALFONSO: Gentlemen, if this really is the custom
    so be it; but I'd rather she didn't.
    I've only just sworn by the sword
    to defend all women:
    and I'd only be offending them
    if I allowed one of them to shoe me.

ELVIRA: Even if I were the most famous woman
    in the whole of Rome
    I would not deserve to come near your feet.
    You would do me the greatest of honours
    by letting me help you with your spurs.

ALFONSO: There's no way round this then?

ELVIRA: None at all.

ALFONSO: Well, get on with it then.

ELVIRA: Your faithful slave humbles herself at your feet,
                                   sire.

ALFONSO: This can't be right;
    you're the eighth wonder of the world.

COUNT: Now sire that you have been made king
    according to the ancient custom of Castile,
    it is your right to give out orders
    and bestow gifts.

ALFONSO: It would be right indeed,
 if only I had anything to give.
 I, a boy king, hounded for ten years,
 who's never had a fatherland, a palace, a fixed home,
 who's always been on the run –
 what could I possibly give when I've always had nothing?
 But now that I hold this sceptre
 and have been given this sword to claim back my kingdom
 let me use it to hunt down the Moors
 and reward you all with what I might win in battle.
DON ESTEBAN: Well spoken, sire.
COUNT: So well spoken, Esteban,
 that the earth itself gives its blessing to his words.
 (*Enter NUÑO.*)
NUÑO: Yes; but why embark on the conquest of foreign lands
 when there is so much war and strife at home.
 Alfonso, claim first of all what is rightfully yours
 and only when that's secure go ahead and attack the Moors.
COUNT: Don Nuño is right, we must concentrate
 at first on what is close at hand.
NUÑO: Let's start off by conquering the castle of Zurita.
 And while we're fighting, the King could take his rest.
ALFONSO: What? The king, stay at home? Do you realise,
              Don Nuño
 what sort of heart lies inside this breast?
 Was it to stay at home that you made me a knight?
 This sword was not made for staying still,
 St James would not have given it to me
 had he not known of its fiery temper.
 This sword, let me tell you, is from Toledo.
 Have you ever seen steel so beautiful?
 A blade like this cuts as sharp as the Tagus;
 it would never dream of staying still
 knowing what I've sworn to do with it.
 And he who knows how to use this sword
 knows also how to surround a castle.
 Come on, those who want to, follow me.
 Let's see what we can do with Saint James's steel!
 (*Exit.*)

COUNT: Have you seen anyone quite as brave as he?
   He's certainly his grandfather's child.
NUÑO: And his heroic father's son.
ELVIRA: The sun to his noble mother's beautiful dawn.
DON ESTEBAN: If his virtue grows with his years
   then this comparison with the sun suits him well.
COUNT: It certainly suits someone so full of goodness.
DON ESTEBAN: Well then, my lords, let's go and follow
                       Alfonso the Good.

(Exit all the courtiers. Enter LOPE and COSTANZA.)

LOPE: Until that time when fiery Mars
   puts down his blood-red orb
   until the flag of war is lowered
   and the stirring trumpets silenced,
   until that time, my lady,
   let me give thanks to
   all the peaceful pleasures
   that love can bring.
   You were upset to see me spoiling for a fight,
   now you see me tender in your arms
   where I hope a few embraces
   will release me from war's pressures.
   Not even all the petals in this garden
   are as plentiful as my feelings
   of eternal love towards you.
   Are you still angry with me for
   having come back to you so hot and flustered?
COSTANZA: Lower your voice, Don Lope,
   someone might be listening to you;
   I know you're only talking to your wife
   and you mean what you're saying,
   but all this stuff about love
   can sound to others rather silly.
LOPE: So there's someone else in the garden?
COSTANZA: Dominguillo entered just a minute ago.
LOPE: Oh, I wouldn't worry about him!
   I brought him up with my very own hands.
   There's not a secret between us.

I go with him everywhere,
he knows everything about me.
Even if you were just a mistress,
he would never betray me
by spreading rumours about you.
He's a true man of honour
despite his lowly birth.

COSTANZA: He's gone away now
after seeing me go all red.
If you want to talk openly about love
it's best done in private.
I once knew a lady so modest
that she thought even the trees were looking at her.
'You're spying on my love life',
she told them,
your leaves are like eyes.

LOPE: Happiness should be shared, they say,
otherwise it's not happiness at all.
There's nothing wrong in giving out
a bit of our love to all one's friends.

COSTANZA: That's all very well, Lope, but some people
are given so much love
that they keep it to themselves.
In life you can't even trust
those closest to you.

LOPE: So you think I'm being insincere
when I talk to you of love?
Surely you must realise that it's you
and not the war that makes me all excited.

COSTANZA: Now I'm really beginning to think
that you were up to no good in Toledo.

LOPE: Oh not that again!
Why is it that whenever love is mentioned
women have to bring in jealousy?
Didn't I just tell you that
it was when I was in Toledo,
trying to get my mind off the war,
that I was seized
by this sudden longing for you.

COSTANZA: It's no use talking to you,
    You've no idea about what I'm saying.
    (*Enter DOMINGUILLO.*)
DOMINGUILLO: Don Lope de Arenas,
    Is this the time for resting in gardens, is it?
    Is this the time for dreaming
    when you should be all alert?
    Is this the time for listening to fountains
    when there's the sound of fifes and drums?
    Is this the time for making birds jealous of your cooing
    when you should be taunting Alfonso with the clash of
                                        steel?
    Is this the time to let yourself be conquered by blind Cupid
    when another boy, of perfect sight, is out to get your
                                        honour?
    Is this the time for carefree thoughts
    when Alfonso's army is carefully obliterating the meadows
    with a horizon so thick with lances
    that the densest of forests cannot match it,
    nor the darkest of wooded mountains?
    I'm amazed that you're even deaf to the horses
    who are neighing to get into your stables.
    Prepare, then, to defend your castle;
    Alfonso may be just a boy, but he's also a Spaniard –
    the first rays of so fierce a sun
    could be strong enough to burn you.
LOPE: What's all this foolishness, Dominguillo?
    You've been around long enough
    to know that not even the most determined of men
    can do much against a fortress like this.
    You make me laugh, you do,
    you're children, the pair of you,
    he for daring to go against me,
    and you for telling me to be on my guard.
    He might have a great future ahead of him,
    but now's not the time for some siege of Troy.
    Alfonso can't be blamed for his audacity,
    his boyishness explains everything.
    As for his counts and vassals,

I laugh at them for bringing him along.
Listen to all those noisy, drumming soldiers.
Within a couple of months, I bet,
you won't hear a sound out of them,
they'll be longing for Toledo,
a good rest and a filling meal.

COSTANZA: You must know that this fortress
has never ever been taken.

DOMINGUILLO: Was I so wrong in voicing my fears?

LOPE: No, you weren't; but it's still not right
for the frightened to try and frighten off
someone who's just won himself fame and honour.
Come Costanza, come with me.

COSTANZA: I could defend this fortress on my own,
and I'm only a woman.

DOMINGUILLO: I'm sure you could, my lady.

COSTANZA: Give me a sword and a shield!

LOPE: To the battlements, Costanza, to the battlements!
(*Exit LOPE and COSTANZA.*)

DOMINGUILLO: With his beloved Costanza by his side
he thinks he's all safe in his fortress,
but little does he know
that today I'll be going over to the King,
and she'll be going into mourning,
and he'll be off to his tomb.
I know the fortress has a little gate
where I can come and go unnoticed,
and make my way to the castle forecourt.
He'll soon know what it's like
when a tumour is lodged inside a body
and a thief inside a house.
(*Enter a group of soldiers with drums and flags, the COUNT,
DON ESTEBAN, NUÑO, ALFONSO, with a ruff and a
sceptre, and PEDRO DIEZ, a soldier.*)

ALFONSO: Let's pitch camp here.

NUÑO: He's the perfect leader!

COUNT: No doubt about it.

ALFONSO: The other place had no grass or water,
we couldn't have stopped there.

NUÑO: He's right about everything.

DON ESTEBAN: Some god must be guiding him.

ALFONSO: I'm sure Lope de Arenas is relying
    too heavily on his castle's reputation.

NUÑO: Look, he's already on the battlements.

DON ESTEBAN: Well, at least his soldiers are,
    together with a most beautiful woman;
    he's certainly confident
    that he's well protected.
    (*COSTANZA appears behind an opening in the battlements.*)

ALFONSO: Is it safe, most warlike lady,
    to come and talk to you.

NUÑO: Don't go so close.

DON ESTEBAN: Of course he can, he's being called;
    Lope's not a person to deceive or betray,
    he's only acting like a gentleman
    and paying his due respects.

ALFONSO: I've dared
    to come close enough to hear your voice
    for I can see you're a queen among women,
    and I can always trust women like you,
    I swear to God.

COSTANZA: You act just like a king.

ALFONSO: What's your name?

COSTANZA: I'll tell you mine,
    if you tell me yours.

ALFONSO: I'm the King.

COSTANZA: I must congratulate you.

ALFONSO: I'm offended by your congratulations;
    I'm not a king since yesterday;
    I've been one since birth.

COSTANZA: Your majesty, I was not congratulating you on
                                    your birthright
    but on your sword and sceptre, and first campaign.
    Surely I was right in doing so?

ALFONSO: You were completely right, my lady;
    and, believe me, how sorry I am
    to see you on the battlements.

COSTANZA: Why, do I look that bad?

ALFONSO: Not at all, in fact the sight of you
    filled me at first with joy.
    It's just that I don't
    like to see a woman acting as a soldier.

COSTANZA: So you don't take me seriously then?

ALFONSO: When I was made a knight,
    I promised to defend all women;
    so if I fight against one,
    I'm breaking my vow.

COSTANZA: You've got lovely manners for someone your
                                                    age;
    kings must be born with grey hairs.

ALFONSO: I feel as if I'm hearing
    sweet murmurings from behind the castle's walls.

DON ESTEBAN: This is no time for flirting with women.

ALFONSO: Tell me who you are,
    if you think it's right to do so.

COSTANZA: I'm Don Lope's wife.
    (*She steps out into the open.*)

ALFONSO: You've been together for many years.

COSTANZA: Many more years than you yourself have lived.

ALFONSO: But how could he then involve you
    in the affairs of war?

COSTANZA: Perhaps he thought that a woman
    would be a good enough defence
    against a child conqueror.

ALFONSO: He's put too much trust in his good name,
    but that's not enough to protect
    either his walls from my sword
    or his honour from my person.

COSTANZA: If you're not disputing that he's an honourable
                                                        man,
    why bother to use your sword against his walls?

ALFONSO: I wouldn't test my patience too much, if I were
                                                        you;
    you don't know the sort of person you're dealing with;
    I already feel the man in me emerging.

COSTANZA: There's no need to get so angry.
ALFONSO: You're quite right.
  But, as you've come to talk to me,
  and I must keep my vow,
  we'll have to think more seriously
  about the terms for peace.
COSTANZA: I've thought of a solution.
ALFONSO: And what is that?
COSTANZA: You must send one of your knights inside
  to talk directly to Don Lope.
  I'll guarantee his safety.
ALFONSO: And who shall it be?
NUÑO: I could go myself.
ALFONSO: Go then.
NUÑO: I'm off.
COSTANZA: And I, sire, will go to warn Don Lope.
  (*Exit NUÑO and COSTANZA.*)
ALFONSO: I must be in love,
  I found my whole manner
  softening when I was with her.
COUNT: There's no place for such tenderness in a soldier.
ALFONSO: I've too little experience of war to know that.
  All I can say is that she's impressed me deeply.
  (*Enter DOMINGUILLO.*)
DOMINGUILLO: Let me through.
SOLDIER: Wait there!
ALFONSO: What's all this?
SOLDIER: One of Lope's men has come to see you.
DOMINGUILLO: It isn't just the desire to see you
  that has brought me here
  but my sense of duty and love for my king.
ALFONSO: I appreciate your motives.
  What do you want?
DOMINGUILLO: Listen, sire:
  if I give you this castle
  will you provide me with food?
ALFONSO: Yes
DOMINGUILLO: King's honour?

ALFONSO: Yes;
    but tell me your name.
DOMINGUILLO: Me? I'm Dominguillo.
ALFONSO: You seem a man who lives off his wits.
DOMINGUILLO: I'm Lope's confidante;
    but it's his trust in me
    that'll prove his ruin, sire.
    I want to give you the fortress;
    with me on your side
    you'll achieve more in a month
    than you might do in ten years.
ALFONSO: You?
DOMINGUILLO: Yes, sire.
ALFONSO: How?
DOMINGUILLO: By killing Lope de Arenas.
ALFONSO: But how can that be
    if he's your lord?
DOMINGUILLO: I can't have a lord who's a traitor
    and denies you this castle.
    It's you who's my king.
ALFONSO: That is so;
    but how are you going to
    get back inside and be trusted
    now that they've seen you out here?
DOMINGUILLO: If you allow me to injure one of your
                                soldiers,
    – not fatally, of course, I'll be very careful –
    then I could claim that I came outside
    to carry out this deed.
COUNT: This is a rather strange request.
ALFONSO: Is there any one of you soldiers
    who wants to be injured by this man?
DON ESTEBAN: Just for the fame and glory of it,
    I imagine that someone will volunteer.
COUNT: Well, what's a little dagger wound to one of you?
ALFONSO: Quite a lot, it seems,
    they're all turning the other way and trembling.
PEDRO DIEZ: If the fortress means so much to you
    I don't mind a little wound,

I'll even die if you wish.

Come on, let's get it over with.

ALFONSO: Where are you from?

PEDRO DIEZ: From Toledo.

ALFONSO: I should have known.

COUNT: Where else would you find a man without fear?

Tell me your name, soldier.

PEDRO DIEZ: They call me Pero Diez.

DON ESTEBAN: Lope's standing on the battlements.

ALFONSO: Praise God for making such a brave man!

I won't forget you.

Go on and wound him, Dominguillo;

Lope's looking at you from the castle.

DOMINGUILLO: You want to go through with this?

PEDRO DIEZ: Of course I do.

DOMINGUILLO: Where do you want it?

PEDRO DIEZ: In the head,

you rogue.

DOMINGUILLO: Drop your sword!

PEDRO DIEZ: No way, you must be joking.

DOMINGUILLO: Come here, you fool, take that!

PEDRO DIEZ: Son of a bitch!

COUNT: Go and get him.

DOMINGUILLO: My lord, open the gate;

I've just killed a man.

DON ESTEBAN: You traitor!

LOPE: Open up!

SOLDIER: (*Inside.*) Get in.

LOPE: Close it.

SOLDIER: (*Inside.*) I'm closing it.

(*LOPE comes down from the battlements.*)

DON ESTEBAN: Well that was a good piece of acting.

COUNT: What a clever man!

ALFONSO: He's reckless.

DON ESTEBAN: We need a doctor,

The injury scene was overdone.

ALFONSO: You know what I'm thinking Pedro?

Though I was born a king,

41

I'd like at this very moment
to be in your position,
to have done what you did.
What's more, I'd rather have
that wound on my head
than the crown you see me wearing.
Let me tell you, loyal Pedro
that your worthy wound
is the crimson ribbon
for you to tie a laurel wreath.
These gashes on your forehead
are worth more to me than the fortress gates;
I can't bear to see your gushing blood,
for there's nobility in your veins, I'm sure.
Your name means Ten, I've noticed.
Bring me your shield,
and with my ten fingers
I'll multiply your wound ten times,
With your blood, my two hands
will make ten crimson bars
that shall always be the coat of arms
of the Diez family from Toledo.
(*ALFONSO dips his fingers in the blood and makes ten marks
on the shield.*)
These bars glitter in the light,
They'll turn a battlefield to silver.

PEDRO DIEZ: There's one thing you can be sure of,
    this blood will never be disloyal;
    and the man who offered you his life today
    will offer it a thousand times to come.

ALFONSO: Get your wound seen to.

COUNT: If I'd been told such a story
    about Alexander the Great
    I wouldn't have believed it.
    May God protect you for a thousand years.

DON ESTEBAN: I think we've had proof enough
    of the man's nobility
    and zealous piety.
    As for you, sire,

it's time for you to rest:
you can be sure now that the castle's yours.
ALFONSO: I hate the idea of having had to pay for it
with the blood of a nobleman.
COUNT: Remember, you're a soldier;
you shouldn't reveal such tender feelings
ALFONSO: I know you're right,
I must never show any pity.
Nor any love.
(*They all leave, enter DOMINGUILLO and LOPE.*)
LOPE: A brave performance, Dominguillo.
DOMINGUILLO: I wanted the King and his followers to
know
that a simple man like myself,
risen from nowhere,
employed as your jester,
is as capable of great deeds
as the best-paid of soldiers.
LOPE: No-one could accuse you now of being a nobody.
I had never thought of you as being so brave.
DOMINGUILLO: If I had to I would even place my hands
in the fire
and pretend I was laying them on flowers.
LOPE: I bet the King was devastated.
DOMINGUILLO: He's bound soon to lift the siege.
LOPE: You're a good man.
I wasn't wrong to have loved you
or to have entrusted you with my life.
DOMINGUILLO: Don't fool yourself.
I've done what I could,
but there's not much more I can do
if the siege goes on longer than a day.
LOPE: I was thinking today of having a shave.
DOMINGUILLO: You're beginning to worry me, sire;
Alfonso's hammering at the gate,
and yet you've time for such trifles.
LOPE: That man whom the King has sent as an ambassador
is a spy who thinks I'm unflustered by the sound of drums.
Let's not disillusion him.

Bring him in,
I want him to see me being shaved.
DOMINGUILLO: Go in there, sire,
and I'll make sure that Don Nuño
is astounded by your lack of nerves.
(*Exit LOPE.*)
How could I have planned this better?
His fate now is more firmly sealed,
than if he were already in his shroud.
Has ever a man died before
while lying on the mortuary slab?
The barber has arrived...
now he's sitting in the chair...
What I am waiting for? What's up with me?
Not only have I got him by the short and curlies
but by the beard as well.
Let's seize this hairy moment!
Over there, in the corner, I see a spear.
May heaven help my aim,
I'll try and get him in the back
and pierce him to the heart.
Then, whatever happens,
I'll have to exit fast.
(*He throws the spear.*)
LOPE: (*From within.*) Holy Mary Mother of God, help me!
DOMINGUILLO: I've got him through the shoulders.
What am I waiting for?
(*Exit DOMINGUILLO.*)
BARBER: (*From within.*) I've never seen such evil!
Please, everyone, soldiers,
come here fast,
the traitor is running off!
(*Enter NUÑO, soldiers, LOPE, with a spear through him,
and COSTANZA.*)
NUÑO: What's happening?
LOPE: Dear, dear Nuño,
this is the ugly deed of a traitor,
only the most common of men
could have done such a thing.

COSTANZA: You refused to listen to me;
    I told you not to trust him.
LOPE: But I loved him, my lady,
    I would never have thought evil of him.
    My voice is weakening by the moment.
    It's only fair that I should die,
    and let the King have his castle.
    Here, Nuño, take this key,
    take it in my name;
    forgive me for what I have done,
    you know I had no other choice.
    I went against the King,
    but I stayed true to my oath,
    my duty is now accomplished.
NUÑO: He's dead.
COSTANZA: His only crime was to have trusted a traitor,
    he was never one himself.
NUÑO: Take him away. I can't wait any longer,
    I must rush to tell the King the news.
    (*LOPE is carried off. Exit NUÑO.*)
COSTANZA: What sort of justice is this
    that allows a man to die
    simply for trusting a man unworthy of him
    and doing so only out of love?
    Don Lope, loyal friends can do great good,
    but you must chose them well –
    they must have nobility in their souls.
    There is no greater punishment
    for a man of truth and honour
    than false friendship;
    anyone can guard against an enemy
    but not against a so-called friend.
    (*Enter ALFONSO, the COUNT, DON ESTEBAN,
    DOMINGUILLO and retinue.*)
ALFONSO: How much she must have suffered!
NUÑO: There's no consoling her.
ALFONSO: Costanza, when I spoke to you
    from the other side of the battlements,

I never knew that I would be here so soon
nor could you have imagined your present grief.
COSTANZA: I've nothing to say about
your taking of the fortress;
these are matters of war,
and women don't understand them;
everyone who fights
believes theirs is the just cause.
You might show sympathy for me
as I mourn my husband;
but you don't realise how much sadder you make me
by treating so generously
the despicable man who killed him.
I'm sorry, I have to go now,
I can't hold my tears back any longer.
COUNT: She is absolutely right;
but you've taken the fortress,
and you've got to keep your word.
Give the man the reward
that you have promised.
ALFONSO: We'll have to decide now
what exactly we owe him.
DON ESTEBAN: Two thousand maravedis a year,
your majesty,
I think would suit him nicely
ALFONSO: Very well, don Esteban, so be it.
I'll make that his pension.
But I'll also make sure that
he'll never slander or kill
another trusting person.
Take out his eyes!
DOMINGUILLO: Sire! ...
ALFONSO: There's no use protesting.
DOMINGUILLO: That's a great way of earning a couple
of grand!
NUÑO: A thousand maravedis for each eye.
What more do you want?
DOMINGUILLO: You call yourself a king? You're a tyrant!
ALFONSO: Do you want to lose your life as well?

DOMINGUILLO: Is this the way a king behaves?

ALFONSO: What's more, you're getting two rewards not one.
    For your act of treachery I'm paying you well,
    for being a traitor I'm paying you badly.

DOMINGUILLO: You're just like your father and your
                                            grandfather.

ALFONSO: They would have done the same as me.
    The man whom you wounded
    I appoint Lord of Zurita,
    and I'll offer him the hand of Costanza,
    if she so wishes.

DOMINGUILLO: I too have been a faithful servant
    but I no longer want to be rewarded
    now that I know that my reward is to be punished.
    I have just one favour to ask –
    spare me one of my eyes.

ALFONSO: Eyes off, I say!
    Even if you had two thousand,
    I'd have each one removed,
    for you did as much
    to the man who raised you
    and treated you so well.
    (*Exit ALFONSO and his noblemen.*)

FIRST SOLDIER: Calm down, brother, there's no need to
                                    get in such a state,
    just think, you'll never have to worry again about food.
    Eat and shut up. What on earth's the matter?

DOMINGUILLO: I want to see if what I'm eating is clean,
    it's no good eating if you can't see the food.

SECOND SOLDIER: If you avoid eating meat pies,
    and don't buy anything ready cooked,
    you'll have nothing to worry about.

DOMINGUILLO: And you call that reassurance?

FIRST SOLDIER: The King pays your rent,
    and all you do is to go on about your sight.

DOMINGUILLO: Do you think I really wanted this?
    Is there anyone who would have done the same
    for two thousand maravedis?

SECOND SOLDIER: Get going, brother, and stop all that
crying.

DOMINGUILLO: Is that it, then? You're abandoning me...

FIRST SOLDIER: What's the choice?

DOMINGUILLO: ...without even a good night?

End of Act One.

ACT TWO

*Enter DON ILLÁN, son of DON ESTEBAN, and GARCERÁN
MANRIQUE, son of the COUNT.*

ILLÁN: Tell me, Garcerán,
   all that's happened in these years.
GARCERÁN: There's no time now;
   we'll have a long talk later.
ILLÁN: There's surely time for something
   before the King and Queen arrive;
   they're bound to be late,
   the festivities will have held them up.
GARCERÁN: Listen carefully, then:
   I'll try and give the briefest summary,
   forgive me if this becomes too long.
   Let's start from the beginning.
   When King Alfonso VIII had taken Zurita castle,
   after the murder of Don Lope de Arenas,
   my dear father Count Manrique,
   Alfonso's loyal and trusted guardian,
   went off with his men to pursue his feud
   with Fernán Ruíz de Castro,
   supporter of the King's uncle, Ferdinand of Leon.
   Caught off his guard in a field,
   while changing his armour,
   he was killed by his enemy.
   I was living at the time near Burgos,
   where I had been working for over ten years
   in the service of the King.
   I was no ordinary page,
   raised among pageants and luxuries:
   I was brought up at Alfonso's side,
   a sword always at the ready
   to conquer the rebelling armies of his land.
   Eventually, when Alfonso seemed at last
   to be rid and venged of Ferdinand of Leon,
   he was roused by stories of the Holy War

to cross the seas and head out East
and help the greatest soldiers of his day.
So he joined the crusade led by Richard the Lion Heart,
who travelled over half of Asia
to protect Christ's Sepulchre at Jerusalem.
I was with Alfonso wherever he went
until that glorious day, on the fields of Bethlehem,
when the Saracens were defeated by the English king.
To reward Alfonso for all his valiant deeds
Richard offered him the hand of his daughter Leonor,
whose virtues had been widely praised.
Then we returned, Illán, to Spain,
from where I went to London with two prelates
to bring the lady to Burgos for her wedding;
this, as you know, has just been celebrated in festivities
that dazzled all the many guests from England and Spain.
Alfonso comes now to Toledo with a fame so great that
the African barbarians tremble at the mention of his name.
Here he will try and gather his finest men
and go on to Cordoba and Seville,
to fight against Zulema and Ben Caid:
his horses quench their thirst today in the Tagus,
tomorrow they'll be drinking water stained with Moorish
blood.

ILLÁN: The King and Queen are here, you better stop;
we'll talk again some other time.

GARCERÁN: I'll always be at your service, Illán,
for it was Don Esteban, your father,
who gave me the sword I carry still.
He knighted me in Galicia,
next to the altar of Saint James.
(*Enter a procession of knights, followed by King ALFONSO,
now an adult, and his wife LEONOR, whom he holds by
the hands.
They are accompanied by DON BLASCO.*)

BLASCO: Toledo offers you these keys, noble King,
and her citizens their souls;
we whose love for you will always grow

humbly kiss your royal hands.
And you, fair queen, whose shining face
reflects all the glory of the French and English kings,
may you be fortunate in your offspring.
As for your own virtues,
I can only compare these to the rays of sun
that crown this most beautiful of dawns.

ALFONSO: I am deeply indebted for all you have done
for me,
and promise that from now on I'll extend Toledo's walls
and grant the city greater privileges.

BLASCO: You will be strengthening our walls with loyalty
and faith.

ALFONSO: What do you think, Leonor,
of this famous city?

LEONOR: I've never seen any place like it,
so strong and noble in appearance,
so steeped in honour.
But I've yet to find in Castile
or indeed in the whole of Spain,
a place worthy to be your throne.
Not even, dearest Alfonso,
all the many wonders I saw on our wedding day
can compare with what I see in you.

ALFONSO: Leonor, I swear with all my heart –
and I would have said the same even
were we not joined in holy matrimony –
that had I seen Troy in her freedom,
Greece at her noble best,
Rome at her most powerful,
Spain in her ancient honour
I too would not have seen
a sight equal to what I see in you.

ILLÁN: Let me kiss the feet of Your Highness.

ALFONSO: I want to introduce you to Don Illán,
a Toledan of purest blood
whose father's memory does this city proud.
On the ceiling behind this cathedral's choir,

you will find his father portrayed
as an armoured knight on horseback –
a worthy memorial to this brave Christian soldier.
ILLÁN: Here, my lady, if you look above you now,
before you reach the choir,
you'll see the work to which the King refers.
LEONOR: His noble aspect seems to be copied in yours,
the two of you are pillars of this city.
ILLÁN: May God bless you a thousand times.
ALFONSO: Garcerán...
GARCERÁN: Sire.
ALFONSO: I want this afternoon to visit the banks of the
Tagus.
GARCERÁN: You must allow me beforehand to
arrange for some shelter,
the sun will be very hot;
the famous palace of Galiana –
the Moorish beauty who seduced Charlemagne –
is still there, but it's roof has fallen in.
ALFONSO: Then we'll have to repair it immediately.
GARCERÁN: The Tagus has swollen and surrounded
most of the palace with water.
Probably no-one has slept there since Galiana's time.
ALFONSO: We'll go down there all the same.
GARCERÁN: Even if the river is unwilling,
I'll bend her to your desires.
ALFONSO: Let's go, my lovely Leonor.
LEONOR: Here I am, pliant to your every wish.
ALFONSO: You're so kind to me.
I don't understand how you put up with all my loving.
Your virtue must be offended by it.
LEONOR: How could I possibly be offended?
Such love is natural between a husband and his wife.
ALFONSO: Remember what I asked, Garcerán.
GARCERÁN: I'll be thinking of nothing else.
ILLÁN: The King and Queen are rather flirtatious today.
GARCERÁN: She's certainly a great beauty,
and he's a born seducer.

(*Exit everyone, enter RACHEL, the Jewish woman, and
SIBILA, her sister.*)

RACHEL: What did you think of Leonor?

SIBILA: For a foreigner, Rachel,
    she's beautiful alright.

RACHEL: Did you really find her attractive –
    that snow-queen from the north?
    There must be something about her icy glance
    that freezes the judgement of those who look at her.
    Oh for some Spanish fire, someone with a real body!
    A body that doesn't burn as soon as the sun comes out,
    that doesn't weaken as the day goes on,
    that's more glorious still in the midday sun.
    Spain is made for love,
    it's a place of passion and sensation
    where Venus can feel at home.
    I'm sure that ancient Cyprus,
    where the goddess came from,
    must have stolen all her beauties from us.
    I know I'm not a Christian, Sibila,
    but I'm a Spaniard; that alone makes me special.

SIBILA: I'm glad you think so, it's a shame the Christians
                                                    don't;
    we Jewesses are hardly known for vivacity or wit.

RACHEL: But that's because we hide our charms.
    If Christians don't like the thought of our blood,
    why should we show them what
    our tongues and hands are capable of?
    As soon as I saw that woman
    going into church with her husband,
    I could see immediately the sort she was,
    despite her lovely face.
    I can tell you now
    that however much Alfonso tries to love her,
    he'll always be pressing his lips against snow.

SIBILA: Can't you see, Rachel,
    that instead of turning you to ice
    she seems to have put you on heat.

That's why you've come down here,
to cool off in the Tagus.

RACHEL: Perhaps you're right;
there could well have been some
fire hiding behind all that snow.

SIBILA: Fire! What do you mean?

RACHEL: I'm sure it's Alfonso who's warming up
that part of me which the Queen has frozen.

SIBILA: That's quite impossible;
when the snow's so cold,
the sun that reflects off it
provides no heat whatsoever.

RACHEL: Alfonso is bound to fall for me.

SIBILA: But he's a king.

RACHEL: Even if he were not,
I would still be wondering
what that passionate soldier
is doing with that frozen angel.

SIBILA: Do you want to have that swim or not?

RACHEL: Yes.

SIBILA: Well, then, let's leave the King and Queen
happily in their little palace.

RACHEL: I don't think anyone will see me here,
surrounded by all these bushes.

SIBILA: Not even the birds will notice you.

RACHEL: I'm surely safe here from love's attentions,
unless love is as furtive as a lynx.

SIBILA: Love is blind in any case.

RACHEL: Not when it comes to seeing what you desire.

SIBILA: Then what's it blind to?

RACHEL: To all the time and dignity that it loses.
Just think of those dirty old men
hiding for hours in the bushes to gawp at the naked
Susanna.
I can really identify with her.

SIBILA: Don't worry, I'll look after you.

RACHEL: Oh, God!

SIBILA: What's wrong?

RACHEL: I thought I saw the King looking at me…
    It was actually quite a pleasant sensation,
    I can't get his image out of my mind.
    (*Enter ALFONSO and GARCERÁN.*)
ALFONSO: I'm so glad to be alone with you here, Garcerán,
    lying by the lovely banks of the Tagus,
    with a gentle breeze rippling the water;
    at last I can tell you what's been troubling me for years.
    Although you're with me all the time,
    I don't feel you can always see what's on my mind.
    A man always carries his face with him,
    but he needs a mirror if he wants to look at it;
    a mirror should be someone like you, a close friend.
    I'm hoping now to find my thoughts reflected in your
                                  advice;
    without your mirror I wouldn't know where to turn to.
    I spent, as you know, a dreadful childhood,
    persecuted in a way unimaginable for someone so young.
    I was barely ten when I put on my first coat of armour,
    took out my sword, and, with God's help, recovered my
                                 kingdom,
    and slowly made up for all that I had suffered.
    I'm married now, I love Leonor, I'm happy on the throne.
    But if I don't enlarge soon my inherited lands
    what sort of legacy will I leave my own children?
GARCERÁN: Love has closed the awful chapter of your past,
    but it should not stop you from fighting on;
    your religion, sire, needs you more than ever,
    for the Moor is almost at your doorstep,
    waving his sword from the Cordoban frontier,
    waiting for the chance to buckle on his spurs,
    the moment you relax and take off yours.
    If you don't do something, he will. Why hesitate?
    If love for your wife has enflamed you so, why be frozen
    to the spot now that what you love is threatened?
    What are you looking at?
ALFONSO: Come here, Garcerán, quick,
    the heavens are certainly taking care of you today!

Can't you see, shining like ice below the crystal surface,
a nymph struggling to cover herself with a veil of water?
Can't you see over there an Ovid poem made flesh –
a naked vision that turns Toledo's banks into Arcadia?

GARCERÁN: I can see her alright and I'm beginning to
shake,
My God, I've never seen such extraordinary beauty;
I can hardly look at her without being overcome with lust.
Was there ever a sculptor who carved out of marble
such a perfect figure, or imagined such snow-white beauty?
She's left me speechless, I've run out of similes.
Hey, sire, sire!

ALFONSO: You're calling me?

GARCERÁN: Yes.

ALFONSO: Well, what do you want?

GARCERÁN: I'm wondering if you're going to go after her.

ALFONSO: She's already drying herself and getting dressed.
I hope that
branch is struck by lighting for handing back her clothes!

GARCERÁN: What! Do you want her to be deprived of
them like Europa was?
Or perhaps you'd like her to wander around these bushes
as in Adam's time, wearing nothing but a smile?
If I were you, I wouldn't use your eyes so much.
Remember what happened to King David
after he gazed at Bathsheba making circles in a pool –
those crystal waters cost him floods of tears.

ALFONSO: Oh, it's getting worse! What a complete disaster!

GARCERÁN: What's wrong? I've never seen someone
change expression so quickly.

ALFONSO: I never thought I would suffer so much pain.

GARCERÁN: Is she a basilisk or something?

ALFONSO: Much worse than that,
much worse than I could ever have imagined.

GARCERÁN: She can't be such a monster after what we
saw at first.

ALFONSO: Can't you see by her clothes why I'm so deeply
troubled?
Can't you see she's a Jewess?

GARCERÁN: Well, if you just want to look at her,
    I don't think her religion is much of a problem;
    of course, if you want something more of her,
    then you should stop doing so this minute.
    Don't get caught up in such an ugly affair.
ALFONSO: Listen, Garcerán. There are two sides to
                           serving a master:
    one is to tell him the honest truth;
    the other is to ensure his pleasure.
    Right now I'd rather you did the latter.
GARCERÁN: I can't believe, sire, that you're going to tarnish
    all your many virtues with a single, ugly error.
ALFONSO: You still haven't understood me.
GARCERÁN: But sire, think how much Leonor adores you.
ALFONSO: I'll say it to you again, Garcerán.
    Put away your moralist's attire,
    and act out the pleasure broker.
    Or else shut up.
GARCERÁN: Don't get angry sire; I'm very sorry.
ALFONSO: She's now fully dressed; tell her I want to
                           speak to her.
GARCERÁN: There's this page whom you know, I'll go
                        and call him;
    he'll be the one to inform her of your love.
ALFONSO: That's absolutely ridiculous!
GARCERÁN: Don't shout, I'll go myself then, if that's what
                        you want.
    Just wait for me here.
ALFONSO: Go.
GARCERÁN: And don't get angry again, you're going to
                        have her.
    (*He goes.*)
ALFONSO: I'll wait for you next to this mulberry tree,
    there's plenty to delight me here.
    The waters that lap against this river's shaded banks
    nurture greater treasures than those
    that are carried by the waves of our Spanish seas.
    Oh seas, you have no cause to be so swollen with pride!
    Though mighty ships ply you in search of the gold

that your cold veins have scattered,
I need only sink my hands into these lush reeds
to uncover something better.
You might be proud of the corral that grows in your womb,
but this can't be compared with the fruit which ripens
by the Tagus's banks and makes the wisest men go crazy.
If you think that mother-of-pearl enriches your beauty,
then wait and see the real pearl that glows in inland waters.
(*Enter BELARDO, a peasant gardener, and FILENO, an
old man.*)

BELARDO: You're a right old comedian, you are!
This is the King's own property,
I'm glad you feel at home;
I wouldn't bother with that notice over there –
it tells even the sun and the air to keep out.

FILENO: What sort of notice is that
which stops people from getting
to where they want to go?
You're wasting your breath on me.

BELARDO: Don't grumble, it makes you look old.

FILENO: If I were in your ragged shoes,
I wouldn't come out with things like that.

BELARDO: Do I really look such a pig's ear?

FILENO: You know you do, Belardo.

BELARDO: If you had the worries I have, Fileno
(and I'm offering them back to the devil,
thanking him kindly for his gift)
you might understand why
I'm looking so terrible.

FILENO: What's been happening to you?

BELARDO: Oh, nothing much.
All the dogs in the area
have declared outright war on me,
that's all.

FILENO: Why's that?

BELARDO: Haven't a clue.
They say they've promised to let me know
once I'm dead.

FILENO: They won't tell you beforehand?

BELARDO: While I'm still alive, I'll try and find out;
once I'm dead, I won't thank them for telling me.

FILENO: Are you sure you've done nothing wrong?

BELARDO: They just envy me, it's as simple as that.

FILENO: Give them a good hiding.

BELARDO: In my whole life,
I've never even hurt a flea;
and I've certainly had the chance to.
The dogs won't achieve anything by biting me;
after causing all this distress,
they'll still be dogs,
and I'll still be a gardener.

FILENO: That's right,
be philosophical about it.

BELARDO: It's getting late.

FILENO: I shouldn't just be standing here,
I've got a real urge to do something
useful with all this wasted space.
Perhaps I'll plant some marrows.

BELARDO: Bye, now.

ALFONSO: Love's a cruel tyrant who spares no-one,
not even those who rule the land;
I can't get this woman from my mind.
I wonder if that peasant know anything about her –
her name, where she lives, her social background.
Hello! What shall I say to him? My good man,
could I interrupt you for a moment?

BELARDO: (*Singing.*) Belardo was a gelardner
in the gardens of Valencia;
life could not have been hardner
had they called him Hortensia.

ALFONSO: I say, do you hear me?
You wouldn't by chance have seen a
young lady coming to bathe here
during her afternoon siesta?

BELARDO: (*Singing.*) When crazy February's over,
he lays down bulbs for May,

hoping he won't be sober
when the spring's all bright and gay.

ALFONSO: Would you please listen?

BELARDO: Who's that?

ALFONSO: You should listen when spoken to,
even if this means stopping what you're doing.

BELARDO: (*Singing.*) I was going, darling mother
to the town of Daimiel
when I missed my path and took another
and ended up in hell.

ALFONSO: If you go on like this,
I'll box you in the ears;
perhaps you'll hear me then.

BELARDO: When a man's at work,
he can hardly hear a thing.

ALFONSO: Yes, especially when he doesn't want to.

BELARDO: What do you wish to know, sir?

ALFONSO: If you've seen today two women
down by the river.

BELARDO: I did, and they are very beautiful;
but, if I'm not mistaken,
they have a certain flaw:
they are Jews, I believe.

ALFONSO: Call them Hebrews, please.

BELARDO: What silliness to lend importance to a name,
at the end of the day, it's all the same.
The world's too full of niceties and pretence,
We prefer fancy words than to give offence.
We use 'our Lord' for God, 'his highness' for a man;
A brazen, shameless strumpet becomes a courtesan.
We call the worst of vices a mere caprice,
we 'cut our resources' when we mean to fleece.
A man without a penny is 'financially distressed',
to be 'a man of honour' is to be elegantly dressed.
'Honest and discreet' serves for 'mean and guarded',
bravery is rashness to the point of being retarded.
Someone 'dark of skin' is often as black as tar,
'healthy competition' is envy when it goes too far.

Anyone who can hold a pen becomes a man of letters,
even if he has a talent which would be better off in fetters;
and as for the tears and shouts of strutting old tarts,
we like to dignify these as the 'performing arts'.
All these many names we can always change at will,
only death is unchangeable when we get the final bill.

ALFONSO: I'm beginning to like you,
despite the roughness of your manner and your metre.

BELARDO: Under this coarse skin,
God has also placed a soul;
in fact we're almost equals.
But, to get back to the question –
what about those two women?
Well, I don't know if they are bad or not;
all I know is that they were swimming.

ALFONSO: But do they come from a good family,
are they well thought of here?

BELARDO: Isn't what you know already enough?
why bother to find out more?
If you've taken a shine to one of them,
and you are, as you seem,
an ambitious man of means,
then my advice is:
keep away from her with a barge-pole.

ALFONSO: I don't want to marry her.

BELARDO: But just imagine having an illegitimate child
with someone of unfortunate birth herself.
What possible good could come of that?

ALFONSO: This peasant is starting to frighten me. (*Aside.*)
Tell me, my friend,
did the women come here on their own
or with company?

BELARDO: Have you ever seen people of their kind
so poor as to go around unaccompanied?
They came by horse and carriage,
with a large group of picnickers.

ALFONSO: You mean, they're wealthy?

BELARDO: Could they possibly be poor?

ALFONSO: Thank God for that!

BELARDO: I'd thank him even more
    if he stopped you from straying;
    if she'd been a Christian,
    you might have been forgiven;
    but as she's…
    polite society would never approve,
    a gentleman like you as well!
    (*Exit BELARDO.*)
ALFONSO: It seems that God
    dispenses his wisdom
    to the most unlikely people.
    Oh what a terrible force is love!
    (*Enter GARCERÁN.*)
GARCERÁN: I've done exactly as I was told,
    that faithless woman who mocks at your religion
    is waiting for you in the old palace.
    She's so much at home there
    she could almost be Galiana,
    if Galiana hadn't become a Christian.
ALFONSO: Don't burden me with religion now, Garcerán.
    The news you bring gives me
    more pleasure than if you'd brought me
    the keys to Granada and Seville,
    or even Mohammed's throne.
    Is she really waiting for me?
GARCERÁN: In the very room I'd laid aside for you.
    She knows you're the King,
    she could hardly have sent her excuses.
ALFONSO: But what shall I do, Garcerán?
GARCERÁN: Just think about the laws you're breaking,
    and remember that a person's greatest victory
    is to conquer his own desires.
ALFONSO: How can I? The memory of
    her beauty haunts me like
    some sublime landscape.
    It's as if a volcano was
    exploding inside me.
    Tell me her name.
GARCERÁN: Rachel.

ALFONSO: It matches her beauty,
    she's as lovely as Jacob's wife.
    But I'm not sure if I have Jacob's fidelity.
GARCERÁN: Jacob stayed fourteen years with his Rachel,
    you don't have to be quite so long with yours.
    You can see her today, and be finished
    with her by tomorrow.
ALFONSO: And why not? I'm only acting
    within a king's rights.
GARCERÁN: I should warn you
    that she has a brother and a father,
    not to mention a servant and some other hag.
ALFONSO: You're not worrying me in the slightest,
    at least she hasn't a bodyguard.
GARCERÁN: You can't reason with love.
ALFONSO: Nor escape its cruelty.
    Wait for me, beautiful Rachel,
    your new lover, Jacob, is coming.
    (*They leave; enter Queen LEONOR and BLASCO.*)
LEONOR: Hasn't Alfonso returned yet to Toledo?
BLASCO: He's probably taking his time
    walking along the river's shaded banks,
    enjoying the sparkling beauty of the waters.
    Or perhaps he's climbed the hill on the other side,
    the view from there is quite superb.
LEONOR: I fear the worst,
    I've never been so worried as I am now.
BLASCO: It seems you're jealous.
LEONOR: Suspicious, certainly.
    I'm sure that something's going on.
BLASCO: You must not think like that,
    suspiciousness is a terrible disease,
    never allow it to cloud your mind,
    even in your more rational moments.
    My master the King adores you;
    you shouldn't stir up trouble
    when everything is calm.
LEONOR: How can I stop myself having these thoughts
    if they're trapped within me?

BLASCO: Some form of entertainment usually helps.

LEONOR: Alright then,
why don't you try to amuse me?
Let's see if that has any effect.

BLASCO: A game of cards might do the trick.

LEONOR: When my mood is as bad as it is today,
cards make no difference whatsoever.
Clara, bring me my writing desk;
and ask a singer to come here.

CLARA: Your love for the King
is turning quickly into madness.

LEONOR: Do you think a day's absence means nothing?
Let me write. Move away from me;
you'll see what I'm doing later.
(*Enter GARCERÁN.*)

GARCERÁN: What's the Queen doing?

CLARA: Can't you see she's writing a letter?

GARCERÁN: I've just been with the King,
we were forced to leave the river path
to attend to some pressing amorous matter.
It's nothing to be worried about,
everything's now in order.

CLARA: Could you tell me where he is, please?

GARCERÁN: He's near.

CLARA: Very near?

GARCERÁN: Oh look, here he comes.
(*Enter ALFONSO.*)

ALFONSO: Hush, don't make any noise.
What's my little Leonor up to?

CLARA: She's writing to console herself for your absence.

ALFONSO: Did she really miss me?

CLARA: So much so that it's a miracle she's still alive.

ALFONSO: Could you leave me alone with her.

GARCERÁN: (*To CLARA.*) I need to speak to you.

CLARA: Let's go.

ALFONSO: (*To himself.*) I want love to tell me what
conclusion
to expect from such a mad beginning.

And I want my soul to reply:
'I've been out of my mind'.

LEONOR: (*Writing.*) I've been out of my mind...

ALFONSO: (*To himself.*) Leonor's responding to my thoughts
down to my very tone of voice.
Fortunately my love for...

LEONOR: (*Writing.*) My love for...

ALFONSO: (*Aside.*) Once again!
Oh my God, this is uncanny,
it must be a bad omen.
I better wait until she's finished
her letter before replying.

LEONOR: (*Writing.*) I haven't seen you since yesterday.

ALFONSO: (*Aside.*) She must be talking to me,
That's doubtlessly her way of
trying to forget my absence.

LEONOR: (*Writing.*) I am terribly unwell...

ALFONSO: (*Aside.*) Oh no, she's about to reveal
what she's suffering from!

LEONOR: (*Writing.*) I am sickening from jealousy.

ALFONSO: (*Aside.*) It's all over for me!
She must have her spies,
she seems to know everything.
What's she going to do?

LEONOR: (*Writing.*) I'm surely going to die,
my fears are so great.

ALFONSO: (*Aside.*) Don't let my thoughts delude you further;
ever since that basilisk set eyes on me,
I haven't been myself at all.
What a strange form of torment!

LEONOR: (*Writing.*) The pain of jealousy is so strange!

ALFONSO: (*Aside.*) It's high time I replied.
I must say something to give back her...

LEONOR: (*Writing.*) Peace of mind.

ALFONSO: I can't wait a moment longer. (*Aside.*)
Leonor, what's this?

LEONOR: Sire!

ALFONSO: Whom are you writing to, Leonor?

LEONOR: To you, as you've been away.

ALFONSO: Me? Been away?

LEONOR: Yes, since yesterday.
Isn't that being away?

ALFONSO: No, my lady;
I might not have been in this building,
but I never left you for a moment:
in my mind's eye you were always as close to
me as you are right now; and I was hoping
that you would have felt the same.
What have you written?

LEONOR: Lots of silly little things.
For God's sake!
You've no right to see them.

ALFONSO: Give me the piece of paper.

LEONOR: Read it then; but do me the favour
of tearing it up afterwards.

ALFONSO: (*Reading.*) 'I've been out of my mind during
your absence,
I've no more patience left,
but because my love for you is so great,
what patience do you expect me to have?'

LEONOR: Isn't that enough silliness for one day?

ALFONSO: (*Reading.*) 'I haven't seen you since yesterday;
that's long enough to die of love!
A thousand suspicions torment me,
I'm terribly unwell, in short...'

LEONOR: I was only trying out the pen;
please don't read any more.

ALFONSO: (*Reading.*) 'I'm sickening from jealousy.
If you're any later,
I'm surely going to die,
my fears are so great;
Today, I've been tormenting
myself with thoughts of
every moment of every
day I've ever spent with you.
The pain of jealousy is so strange!

    Please free me now from my deluded imaginings,
    and give me back my peace of mind.

LEONOR: And at that very moment,
    my darling, you came into the room.
    And what has my dear King been doing without me?

ALFONSO: I was never without you, as I've just said:
    I spent so much time thinking about you
    that you were always at my side.
    I'll tell you the details later,
    on a more intimate occasion.
    I'm afraid you'll have to leave me now,
    I can hear people coming.

LEONOR: I can see you're tiring of my love already.

ALFONSO: You don't seem to have taken in
    what I've been saying.
    I could never possibly tire of you,
    you're the very air I breathe.

LEONOR: (*Aside.*) Why does he want to send me out of the
                                  room?
    I'm not happy about this at all.
    Though I hardly dare say this,
    it doesn't seem right
    for a woman to be treated so dismissively
    by the man whom she has just married.
    (*Exit LEONOR.*
    Fanfare from within, enter ILLÁN.)

ILLÁN: Count Nuño Perez is outside the palace, my noble
                                    lord,
    together with more than forty of his battalions;
    these illustrious troops, accompanied by the royal guard,
    are now parading below your balconies in all their finery.
    I beg you, sire, to go out and greet them,
    they know you are newly arrived in Toledo,
    and are anxious to display their loyalty.
    A salute from you would be a fitting gesture.

ALFONSO: (*Aside.*) This is a fine time for war-like matters,
    now that my feelings are engaged in a battle
    in which love stands to gain control

over the divided kingdom of my soul.
Illán, tell the Count to leave me alone.

ILLÁN: What sort of reply is that?
Why are you hiding your face?
Do you want to offend the worthy soldier
who has looked after you since you where a child?
Is that how you treat one of the greatest knights
that Ávila has ever produced?
And I can tell you this:
he is so loyal towards you that he will spill
every drop of his blood in your defence.

ALFONSO: What difference does it make whether he's
            brave or loyal
when I've no desire at present to see his bloody parade?

ILLÁN: Calm down, my lord;
I'll tell him to come back when you're in a better mood.

ALFONSO: Illán, tell Nuño to dismiss his men,
say that something unexpected has happened
which has greatly upset me.
Tell him to put down his sword.

ILLÁN: Enough said: we'll just call this a wasted day.
(*Exit ILLÁN.*)

GARCERÁN: You still haven't learnt to hide your feelings.
Couldn't you have put on some show of happiness,
or said something to try and shield your love-sick heart.
Clara tells me that tears are flowing inside the palace.

ALFONSO: When night comes, which will be soon,
and not a patch of light remains,
I want you, Garcerán, to have two horses ready;
have Rachel wait for me, and make sure
she stays in the fields below the town.

GARCERÁN: Haven't you heard what I've been saying
about this latest attack of jealousy?

ALFONSO: I want her to live down there; my visits to her
will attract less attention.

GARCERÁN: Less visits would be better still.
For God's sake, go now and see the Queen,
and try and cheer her up with a few lies.

ALFONSO: I'm afraid it's getting late, it's time I should be
                                                    leaving.
GARCERÁN: (*Aside.*) What has this woman done to him?
                                        But I'm sure
  he'll tire of her soon; these sudden attacks
  of passion usually end as quickly as they've begun.
  I shouldn't try and stop him, despite my disapproval.
  I'm ready to leave when you are, sire.
ALFONSO: In that case, let's leave immediately;
  I don't think I can control my desires any longer.
GARCERÁN: Then come with me sire.
ALFONSO: Keep close to me, I'm blind you know, and
                                        need a guiding hand.
  (*They leave. Enter DAVID, an old Jew, and LEVI, his son.*)
DAVID: I've been told she's in here,
  and that the King has locked
  the gates so firmly that she cannot leave.
LEVI: You talk about the palace of Galiana
  as if it were a fortress.
  And yet it's been open to the skies
  since the time of the Goths.
DAVID: My son, if the King wants a fortress,
  he will have one wherever he wants;
  and there's nothing anyone can do
  except obey his wishes.
  I imagine he must have eyed your sister from afar,
  and then, like any young man of his position,
  got his servants to fetch her and bring her here.
  Such behaviour doesn't suit a king at all,
  especially when my own daughter's involved.
LEVI: But, father, if that really is what's happened,
  why are we both so worried?
  I mean Alfonso is the King, isn't he?
DAVID: He is, yes.
LEVI: Well, as it's a thankless task
  keeping one's honour
  if we're always prostrating ourselves
  before the humblest Christian,
  then surely we'd be better off

winning favour and respect
in those places where the oppressive laws
against us are issued?
Don't you think it might even be possible
for Rachel to mix her blood with his?

DAVID: As you're very young,
you treat love and other serious matters
as if they were a game.
If you had my white hairs,
you would know that
there s no-one like a king
to raise false hopes.
Leonor will soon find him out,
at first she'll reassure him
by pretending to turn a blind eye
to this love and its nest;
and while the King keeps up his
affair with the faithful Rachel,
Leonor will be searching
for the sword to kill her;
and once one is found,
the King has only to leave
the bed-chamber for a moment
for this sword to make its entry
and penetrate her heart.

LEVI: Old people are always dreaming up tragedies;
these are the melancholy thoughts
caused by the cooling of the blood.
Look, there she is on the balcony,
you can cheer up already.

DAVID: I'll ask this workman
if we'll be allowed through.
(*Enter BELARDO with a sharp-pointed stick.*)

BELARDO: Who goes there?

LEVI: Honest folk.

BELARDO: You've come to steal some fruit.

LEVI: We've only come to talk...

DAVID: Keep your voice down.

LEVI: There s a young woman who's come here…
BELARDO: Is she the one who's never eaten bacon in her
life?
LEVI: Yes.
BELARDO: Well, what do you want her for?
    The stew she made, I can tell you,
    was so incredibly bad and tasteless
    that I doubt if you'll find or eat
    anything quite like it in the whole world.
LEVI: Would it be possible to speak to her?
BELARDO: I don't believe it's permitted to enter the
property…
    But you can always go in if you want to;
    even though it's dark, I can see her quite
    clearly in the light of the stars.
    Get in there.
DAVID: She's shining as brightly as any sun.
LEVI: Come on, father, let's go inside.
    (*Exit DAVID and LEVI.*)
BELARDO: This is a nice little earner the devil's given me –
    guarding a property that has neither a gate nor a fence.
    I've seen everything here in my time:
    picnics, love affairs, quarrelling rivals,
    fist fights, outbursts of jealousy,
    people who come here to swim,
    even people who come to squeeze out their fleas…
    The sky's all covered over there,
    it's beginning to look really threatening.
    Lightning! Some night this is.
    Thunder…! I bet there'll
    be a lover or two thinking
    that the earth's just moved!
    Again! The horses have bolted.
    It's St James running through the sky
    with his shield and sword!
    That's what granny used to say
    every bloody time it stormed.
    Oh what a pissing awful downpour!

if it keeps up like this,
I'm going back to my hovel.
(*Exit BELARDO, enter ALFONSO.*)
ALFONSO: Garcerán has left me,
he went off to get a cape the moment
it began to rain.
But what have I to be frightened of, Rachel?
What can any man fear
who has always the prospect
of paradise in your arms?
My desire for you is so great
that I cannot restrain it at all,
not even if I were offered
more riches than I already possess.
Yet what terrible darkness!
What thunder and lightning!
And the skies are still clear over Toledo.
The heavens seem to be venting
their fury only over these fields;
they must have sensed what I'm up to,
and are punishing and hating me for it.
The clouds speak to me by thundering
and the skies by tearing themselves apart;
they are jealous of my love,
and cry in great sheets of rain.
The flashes of fire are lighting up
the passion within my heart;
the wind is stirring up the dust
to show me that I am blind.
The Tagus is overflowing its banks
to try and put out the flames that engulf me;
but the fire that is love
cannot so easily be extinguished.
The trees are trembling all in a row,
their leaves are shouting out 'Alfonso!',
as if chanting a final wail at a funeral.
Heaven help me! There's an even blacker
cloud that's coming straight towards me,
it looks as if it might break over my head.

(*A sad voice is singing from within.*)

VOICE: King Alfonso, King Alfonso,
    don't say you haven't been warned:
    see how you're losing all the grace
    that God, the greater King, has given.

ALFONSO: I thought I heard a voice inside the cloud,
    it told me that I had upset the Heavens.

VOICE: Think, Alfonso, about your actions.
    Since the time you were a child,
    God has always been your guardian.
    Do not let your lucky star
    be eclipsed now by your lust:
    Remember Roderick, whose insatiable desire
    to enter the secret chamber,
    lost him all his kingdom to the Moors.

ALFONSO: I'm beginning now to understand,
    thank God for that,
    all this is just a trick of Leonor's
    to put me off my appetite.
    I've reached the palace at last;
    I'm going inside. Oh great God above!
    (*The King's on the point of entering when his path is blocked
    by a man with a black cape and a drawn sword and dagger;
    his face is black, and he's mounted on a black steed.*)
    What's this I see in front of me?
    Are you a man? Hello! Tell me who you are!
    Haven't you a voice? He's disappeared already.
    But, why I am so surprised?
    He was just a figment of my frightened imagination.
    I'll go in by the other door,
    and jump over this quiet little stream.
    Oh Lord, protect me!
    (*The shadow returns.*)
    There he is again, that shadow.
    What do you want? Why are you troubling me?
    Who are you?
    (*Enter GARCERÁN.*)

GARCERÁN: I've taken longer than I thought.

ALFONSO: Are you a shadow or are you a man?
    Speak, just say to me 'I'm following you',
    I'm brave enough to take it,
    whether you're dead or alive.
    (*The ghost disappears.*)
GARCERÁN: I heard a voice over there.
ALFONSO: It's gone away again.
GARCERÁN: Who's there?
ALFONSO: Not another shadow!
    But this one spoke with a human voice,
    It said, 'Who's there?'
GARCERÁN: Who's there? Aren't you going to reply?
ALFONSO: A friend.
GARCERÁN: Are you my master the King?
ALFONSO: Yes. Are you Garcerán?
GARCERÁN: The very same. What's wrong with you?
    Why are you trembling?
ALFONSO: I've seen amazing sights.
GARCERÁN: Like what, sire?
ALFONSO: Clouds, ghosts, deafening thunder,
    hail, lightning, celestial music.
GARCERÁN: What fearful omens!
    But what are you doing outside this door?
ALFONSO: I can't get in, every time I try to
    this shadow comes to block my path.
GARCERÁN: You must have offended God,
    we'd better be going back to Toledo.
ALFONSO: Don't be stupid,
    all this is merely trickery.
GARCERÁN: Trickery?
ALFONSO: I know who's behind it too.
GARCERÁN: Look, if there's any magic involved,
    it's surely God who's responsible,
    he's warning you to get away from here.
ALFONSO: You're a coward, Garcerán.
GARCERÁN: Are you really saying that?
ALFONSO: I am.
GARCERÁN: Then I'll take out my sword
    and volunteer to go in first.

ALFONSO: I'll follow you, Garcerán,
    I'm so in love I can hardly think or act,
    I know too well the wrong I'm doing
    but I'll follow you all the same.
    If the senses have to be restrained
    what use is there in having them?
    (*GARCERÁN puts his hand on his sword and enters the palace, followed by the King.*)

End of Act Two.

ACT THREE

Enter ILLÁN and BLASCO.

ILLÁN: The Queen sent me this note, Don Blasco,
    asking me to come here in secret to the Alcazar.
BLASCO: She wrote the same to me, Illán,
    that's why I wasn't anticipating company.
    What can she want from us?
ILLÁN: Some cure, no doubt, for Alfonso's malady.
    (*Enter BELTRÁN the Red.*)
BELTRÁN: May the heavens protect you, good knights.
ILLÁN: What a surprise! Beltrán the Red as well!
BELTRÁN: I wasn't expecting to find anyone here;
    when the Queen sent me this note,
    she told me not to tell a soul.
BLASCO: We were both told the same.
    Do you know what she wants from us?
ILLÁN: I can only think she needs
    someone to moan to about her misfortunes.
    (*Enter GARCERÁN.*)
GARCERÁN: I'm late as usual. Gentlemen, what a surprise!
BLASCO: God be with you, Garcerán Manrique.
BELTRÁN: (*Aside.*) If he's been invited, the Queen won't be
    talking about Alfonso, that's for sure.
    He's the King's most trusted companion,
    he has colluded all along in this sordid affair.
GARCERÁN: I'm astounded to find you lot here,
    unless we've all come for the same reason;
    when the Queen handed me this note
    she insisted I came here on my own.
ILLÁN: She said the same to everyone.
GARCERÁN: Then, this really is some sort of conspiracy.
BELTRÁN: Quiet now, our beautiful Queen is entering the
                                   room.

(*Enter the Queen and her young son ENRIQUE, both of
them dressed in mourning.*)

BLASCO: You're in mourning? For whom, my lady?

LEONOR: I don't think, Don Blasco, that much imagination
is needed to know the cause of my distress.
Could you go and lock the doors of this hall.

BELTRÁN: They're already locked. Sit down, your majesty,
and tell us why we have been called here.

ILLÁN: (*Aside.*) She looks so sad!

GARCERÁN: (*Aside.*) I can hardly bear to look at her!
(*The Queen sits down.*)

LEONOR: Noble Blasco de Guzmán,
valiant Beltrán the Red,
Illán, hero of Toledo,
and, last, but not least,
Garcerán Manrique, whose
bravery in the Crusades
is known to every Spaniard –
I think of you four
as the pillars of this kingdom,
the virtues that adorn it;
and, because of this,
I have asked you here today in secret
to propose a quick solution
to this unfortunate affair.
Alfonso, whom we had called the Good,
is, as you know, losing his good name
through a deranged passion.
For seven years now he has locked himself away
with that beautiful Jewess,
whose appeal seems as irresistible
and destructive as Roderick's secret chamber.
He has forgotten who he is;
he's lost all interest in his kingdom,
his life, his fame, and his honour.
Rachel is the one who rules, it's
Rachel who wears the crown of Castile,
who decorates our soldiers
and ennobles our commoners.
She punishes, she locks away,

and does so with such zeal
that in seven whole years
she has not granted a moment's liberty
to her prize prisoner, your King.
What a shameless captivity!
Why, you must be thinking,
do I not talk to him about
the hurt he's causing me as a wife?
I could easily do so, I'm in the right;
but in this respect my feelings
are so repressed that
not a word about my sorrow
has ever issued from my lips.
I've tried speaking with my tears,
but what can voices of water do
against the rocks of his deaf ears?
Yet it's not my personal grief that
troubles me most; it's knowing
how much his sin has angered God,
who's already taking his revenge.
The Moors are advancing from the south,
they who once trembled in Alfonso's shadow,
have dared to leave Granada and Archidona.
Now that they've taken Almodóvar,
they're crossing the Sierra Morena,
and marching freely across La Mancha,
to set up camp in Ciudad Real.
At this rate, Castillians,
they'll soon be at the waters of the Tagus,
with their horses lapping your blood;
soon they'll have breached these walls
and replaced our red flags
with their blue banners;
soon the holy cathedral which
was visited by Our Queen in Heaven
will be desecrated with Mohammed's bones.
How, I want to ask, can you allow a
woman to destroy you in this way?
What's wrong with you all?

Is there really the blood of Goths in you?
Are you really descended from those
noble-blooded soldiers who captured this
city that is the pride of Europe?
Are you Blasco de Guzmán?
Are you Illán, you who are wiping
out the memory of your father Esteban?
He was the one who placed Alfonso in Toledo,
you're the one who's getting rid of him
by consenting to such infamy and dishonour.
And you, are you Beltrán the Red?
All that's red about you is the blush of shame
at all the public discomfort the King's provoking.
And as for you, Garcerán Manrique,
the returning hero from Asia,
can't you see that you're the one
whom everyone is blaming for this torrid affair?
You're the one who's helping your master
instead of taming him as he rampages
like a wild beast through every vice.
Tell me: what's corrupted you?
Has your blood also been tainted by a Hebrew strain?
Well then, all you hot-tempered Spaniards,
I come here today with my son Enrique
to offer you one last chance to prove your mettle:
you must kill the traitress.
If you do not, then you have neither hands,
nor strength, nor honour, nor true blood;
and my son and I will be forced to
to go to England, where we hope we'll have
a better welcome at the pious house of Richard.
(*She leaves.*)
BELTRÁN: My Lady...!
BLASCO: My Queen...!
GARCERÁN: My noble lady...!
ILLÁN: Stop her, for God's sake!
ENRIQUE: You worthless lot!
    Why should she be stopped

when you're incapable and unwilling
to do anything about that vile woman?

ILLÁN: I'll have you know, Prince,
that none of us here is worthless.

ENRIQUE: In my eyes you all are
for exposing me to that woman:
she'll end up like that slave-girl Agar,
giving birth to another bastard Ishmael,
who'll want to kill me when he grows up.

GARCERÁN: Sire, what can we do,
as Alfonso, your father,
is also our King?

ENRIQUE: Acknowledge at least that my mother
is wife to this Alfonso.
Only worthless people could
behave as basely as you do!
How could you not take out
your swords this minute?

BLASCO: Sire, you should treat us better.

ENRIQUE: A great use your grey hairs have been!
It's certainly not wisdom that has
given you a snowy mantle for a beard!
For God's sake, Blasco de Guzmán,
try and live up to your name a bit better!

GARCERÁN: What's this boy going to be like
if he ever reaches manhood?

ILLÁN: He's in the right, Garcerán.

ENRIQUE: How noble of you!

ILLÁN: Sire, let me just tell you...

ENRIQUE: Tell me what, Illán?
Why tell me anything at all
if all I can see is that
my mother's dying of shame,
and my father's buried in it?
You must have some hidden reason
for wanting to defend this Hebrew woman.

ILLÁN: Me, sire?

ENRIQUE: Yes, you.

ILLÁN: My blood is pure, sire, I swear to God!
  In the same way that you were born to a king,
  I am the offspring of emperors, no less:
  This blood that I stand up for
  is inscribed in the annals of antiquity;
  my name of 'Illán of Toledo' comes from
  being descended from the very first Toledan.
BELTRÁN: Look sire, it is neither fear nor guilt
  that makes us put up with this affair;
  but a king is a king, and that is that.
  You must learn to hide your discontent.
ENRIQUE: So what do you want me to do, Beltrán the Red?
BELTRÁN: To turn the other cheek.
ENRIQUE: What a cheek! Keep my face out of this,
  if I were you: if the King's face is a mirror,
  as you all seem to think, then so is mine –
  a mirror to show you all how ugly you are.
  I'm telling you one last time:
  you'll never see me nor my mother again
  unless you kill my father's Hebrew witch!
  (*Exit.*)
BELTRÁN: That's stunned us all! What did you make of that?
GARCERÁN: Don't look at me! I'm no less shocked than
                                        you are;
  but I'm prepared to carry out the deed.
  How could I, you might ask, raise a sword
  against a woman whose care has been entrusted to me
  by the King, who loves her deeply?
  How could I, you might add, spend so many years
  faithfully following the King in his mistaken path
  and then suddenly turn against him?
  And then there's bound to be one of you who'll say that
  I'm only doing this for my own good – to cover up
  a shameful liaison with her accomplice of a sister.
  Well, I swear by all the noble blood that has been
  poured into my veins, that if I have been guilty,
  at least I have not been led astray by lust.
  I stand humbled and confused before you all,

let me make amends for causing so much offence,
allow me to be the first to take on God's revenge!
BELTRÁN: Garcerán, I have never doubted your pious zeal;
I know that you have always tried to do your best;
no-one here is imputing your great virtues;
but as you and Alfonso have grown up together,
are you surprised that the Queen has had cause for
                                                    jealousy,
and has implicated you so greatly in this whole affair?
To begin with, the King's personal doings
did not matter much to us; but now that Castille
and all of Spain's involved, they have become insufferable.
England, amazed by our negligence, is already
preparing to invade; there's not a single city or town
in the whole kingdom unaware of the King's misdeeds.
It's time to win him back and release him from his captor.
GARCERÁN: This is the only right course for us to take.
I for one shall go and arm myself.
BLASCO: I'll back you up.
ILLÁN: And so shall I.
GARCERÁN: Reason is now my king, I'll put myself in her
                                                    protection.
BELTRÁN: Your loyalty will be an example to the world.
(*They exit, enter ALFONSO, RACHEL and SIBILA.*)
ALFONSO: Have you brought the fishing rods?
SIBILA: The gardener is bringing them.
ALFONSO: What a wonderful start to the summer,
and after such a lovely spring as well.
RACHEL: After all these years of love,
why bother with such silly niceties?
ALFONSO: If you think of love as being a child,
then it has to mature with the years.
Which means that ours is a grown-up love
and cannot say anything that is false or silly.
RACHEL: But if love is so uneventful
that it has to talk about the weather,
then surely it'll bore itself to death.
ALFONSO: I'll never be bored with you, I swear to God!

RACHEL: There's no need for swearing, I fully believe you.

ALFONSO: My feelings for you are even stronger now
then when I first set eyes on you.
You're my lady and my queen,
you're my goddess, you're my only
reason for living; you're everything to me,
you're the ruler of my soul.
Of the two of us, you're the most powerful,
for while I rule over Castile,
you rule over me.
(*Enter FILENO and BELARDO with some fishing rods.*)

BELARDO: Those two are muttering away as usual
besides the river.

FILENO: Could you please explain one thing:
how the fuck did you meet the King?
It beats me how a shy person like you,
who can hardly string a word together,
got talking to a man like him.

BELARDO: I might be shy and simple but I know enough
to have read this book – by some minor author
with a name like Vega – in which it's clearly said
that kings are deities until they open their mouths,
after which they behave more normally, like you and I.
On remembering this I then recognised the King in a man
I'd seen pass this way a thousand times.
On bended knees, I began offering him flowers,
then fruit, then some trouts, then the odd quail or two.
He was so overwhelmed that he gave me a raise in status.
Now my days as a common gardening bore are over,
I'm a royal gardener now, and a boatman and fisherman
to boot.

FILENO: What are the lovers going to do now?

BELARDO: Well, as they've asked for these fishing-rods
I have a hunch they might be going fishing.
And, in case you've been wondering why my boat's
all decked up with flowers, gold silk and a damask awning,
I think they might be going boating as well.

FILENO: Where will they go to?

BELARDO: They have this favourite little spot,
    under the shade of a large rock,
    where they go and have a so-called wash.
FILENO: So you think there'll be a bit of splash and tickle?
BELARDO: There might, and there might not.
FILENO: Don't you ever gossip about them?
BELARDO: If a servant gossips about his master,
    then what will everyone be saying about the servant?
    All I can say is that Alfonso's hasn't
    been quite himself these past seven years.
SIBILA: The fishing rods have come.
ALFONSO: (*To RACHEL.*) Why bother with rods
    when you have eyes such as yours?
    Of course fish are not people,
    no matter how many of them
    are swimming in these waters.
RACHEL: I'll be happy just with one of them.
ALFONSO: Put the bait on the hook that
    the heavens gave you as your eyes,
    and see what you can do now.
RACHEL: That's enough of your gallantries for one day,
    you re overdoing the metaphors,
    they're beginning to sound a bit false.
    I'll be more direct in my response:
    I'm casting this rod in your name.
    (*They cast their rods at the front of the stage, which has grass
    around its sides.*)
ALFONSO: And I'm casting mine in yours.
RACHEL: Darling, can you grant me a little favour,
    just like God granted you Spain?
ALFONSO: What is it, my sweet?
RACHEL: I would like anything you catch to be mine,
    and anything I catch to be yours.
ALFONSO: Is that really all you want?
    I would place the whole world at your feet
    if only it could be reduced to a
    floating sphere that I could lift out
    from the water with my fishing line.

RACHEL: I kiss your hands, my royal darling.
SIBILA: Are they tugging at your line already?
RACHEL: No.
SIBILA: How could they resist!
RACHEL: It's too soon, yet.
ALFONSO: Too soon?
   The fish must be idiots not
   to want to rise to your bait.
SIBILA: Oh look, his rod's begun to stir.
RACHEL: Pull.
ALFONSO: Oh, holy Christ!
   I thought at first I'd really caught the globe!
RACHEL: What is it?
ALFONSO: It looks to me like a skull.
RACHEL: What a horrible thing!
BELARDO: Madam, it's probably just some child's skull
   they've tossed into the river.
ALFONSO: There's nothing to worry about.
RACHEL: I'm frightened, no matter what you say:
   don't you remember, my love,
   how we agreed that anything
   you caught would be mine?
ALFONSO: I can't bear to think of you
   worrying about a silliness like that.
RACHEL: Well, don't be upset any longer;
   you're quite right, the skull doesn't mean a thing,
   it was just an unfortunate accident.
BELARDO: The line doesn't want to let go of it,
it's got itself nicely entwined in the eye-sockets.
RACHEL: I'm feeling a strong pull now,
   it looks as if I might have something for you.
ALFONSO: Harder, harder!
   Whatever's that?
RACHEL: An olive branch.
ALFONSO: An olive branch?
RACHEL: Yes.
ALFONSO: So these hooks pick up branches too?
   It's a pity they don't work with the fish,
   I think we'll have to call it a day.

RACHEL: I'm happy to stop.

ALFONSO: Let's get in the boat then.

RACHEL: I'd rather not,
    what with all those underwater hazards,
    I don't want to enter the river.

ALFONSO: Don't let your lovely head
    give those another moment's thought.
    (*Enter MENDOZA, a servant.*)

MENDOZA: Fernán Ruíz has come to see you, sire.

ALFONSO: You mean Fernán of Castro?

MENDOZA: Yes, sire.

ALFONSO: I love that old man, I've done so since I was a
                                                    child.
    But he was the killer, Rachel, of Garcerán's father.
    When Garcerán finds he's here, there'll be such a fight
    that I could easily lose two of the finest men
    who have ever looked after me.

RACHEL: This could be a good moment to make peace
                                                between them,
    what with this unusual fish you've just been given.

ALFONSO: I'd better accompany him, my darling Rachel,
                                                into the city.

RACHEL: May God go with you.

SIBILA: What are the two of us going to do here?

RACHEL: There's nothing we can do without him.
    And now that he's gone, I beg you to
    return with me to the palace.
    I need a large space to try and quell
    this fire that's burning at my chest.
    I wanted to hold my tears back in front of Alfonso,
    but now he's gone I need to let them out in floods.
    It's not the omen that's making me like this,
    it's my fear of having been a sinner.
    (*Exit the two of them.*)

FILENO: I think she's sad.

BELARDO: That seems a reasonable diagnosis;
    I might be a bit thick, Fileno,
    but, if you ask me, I'd say
    there was something very fishy

about all that fishing business.
You know what? I think that the skull
which the King caught for her
means that she's about to die;
and as for the olive branch that
she fished out of the water for him,
that can only mean that peace
is going to return to this kingdom
the moment Rachel's six feet under.

FILENO: So you don't think the King's going
to be given a large bottle of olive oil?

BELARDO: It's an undisputed fact, Fileno –
and I've had this from the highest authorities –
that an olive branch is a symbol of peace.
And peace, I'm telling you, is a dead certainty
once Rachel's gone. As soon as she's in her grave,
the King will be back with the Queen,
and everyone will pretend that nothing's happened.
And what greater peace is there than when
a husband stops bickering with his wife?

FILENO: Some rather grand-looking types are coming this
way.

BELARDO: What, them? They're just a load of knights.

FILENO: They look as if they're about to have a seizure.

BELARDO: They must have a bone to pick.

FILENO: Some bone!

(*Enter GARCERÁN, BLASCO, ILLÁN, BELTRÁN, and
MENDOZA, the servant.*)

ILLÁN: You've done well, Mendoza,
I wouldn't have expected anything less of you.

BELTRÁN: Today we'll rid ourselves of the Hebrew
calamity who gloats on our misfortune.

GARCERÁN: It's a miracle that the King's
gone off today with Fernán Ruíz.

MENDOZA: And an even greater one that
I was able to deliver the message to him.

BLASCO: By what human law is such an infamous
woman as her allowed to live?

87

BELTRÁN: Has the King gone far?

MENDOZA: Very far;
he'll have left the fields by now.

ILLÁN: Today the venging hand of God
has been placed in our care;
we are the means by which He will
extract a punishment and a warning.

BELARDO: (*Aside to FILENO.*) I'll use the cover of these
reeds, Fileno
to make a runner and go tell Rachel;
all these weapons and commotion,
I can't see any good coming out of them.

FILENO: You're doing the right thing. Go and tell
her that there are suspicious people around.

ILLÁN: Today she'll die for sure,
there's no escape.

GARCERÁN: Even if someone were to warn her,
we'll have her trapped.

BLASCO: Let's surround the building
and block every exit.

BELTRÁN: Let's go, I'll be the one
to strike the mortal blow.

ILLÁN: Only you, and no-one else?

GARCERÁN: Anyone who stays behind is
either a traitor or a coward.
(*Exit all, enter RACHEL and SIBILA.*)

SIBILA: Please stop crying, Rachel.

RACHEL: Oh Sibila, what am I going to do?
I want to go back to Toledo;
I'm terrified of being here on my own.

SIBILA: On your own? With all those servants?
And what about your father and your brother?
Aren't they here too?

RACHEL: Oh God, oh God!
My worries are only getting worse.
When Leonor finally sends
down her bolt of lightning,
all I can do to save myself

is to have more lives.
I should never have let
Alfonso out of my sight today;
when disaster strikes it can
get through the strongest door.
(*Enter BELARDO in an agitated state.*)

BELARDO: Rachel, your beautiful face looks troubled,
I'm afraid you won't feel any better
on hearing what I've come to say.
There are knights outside, with capes and daggers;
these don't seem friendly signs to me,
in fact I'd call them rather hostile.
Everyone is talking in a whisper,
one moment they all stop,
the next moment it's all go;
some move up to the front,
others keep to the rear.
There's not a tree without some
discussion going on behind it;
and, in my humble opinion,
when people act like this in a field,
they're usually at war;
I may be a simple gardener,
but I've learnt a thing or two
in the school of life.

RACHEL: You lovely, honest man,
what are you saying?
What are you telling me?
Knights, and fully armed at that!
Oh God, they cannot be here
just to have some fun.
You must run to the King
as fast as you can,
as if the heavens were covering
the stubbled fields with wheat,
as if sheep were shedding wool
like snow from the sky,
as if the trees were bearing fruit

like the Tagus produces sand.
Tell him to come here now
and free me from all their fury.

SIBILA: I hear voices.

BELTRÁN: (*Offstage.*) Break down the doors!

BELARDO: Fly, my lady.

RACHEL: I can't.

ILLÁN: (*Offstage.*) Let's go on in and kill
this Circe who has charmed our King,
this sorceress who's as evil as Medea!

(*The knights enter with their swords unsheathed.*)

RACHEL: You wouldn't be looking for me, would you?

BLASCO: What do you think?
Is there any other woman who deserves
as many swords as these?

RACHEL: You mean a woman as unfortunate as I am?

ILLÁN: Unfortunate! Whatever makes you say that?
Haven't you enjoyed for seven years the favours of
a king who hasn't spent even an hour of his time
either with his people in times of war
or his wife in times of peace?

RACHEL: That's some form of enjoyment that is,
if all I get from enjoying a king
is to end up as miserable as this!
I only wish that the heavens
had made me love instead a
simple peasant like him!

BELARDO: I'd rather you left me out of this,
I've got enough on my plate as it is.

RACHEL: Oh, love, you re so predictable!
Why do you always have to end in tears?
I put a curse on all your joys!

BELTRÁN: Did you really think all
this would have a happy ending?

BLASCO: Knights, what are you waiting for?
By killing this woman you redeem
yourselves and Spain!

ALL: Kill the beast!

RACHEL: I die in the name of Alfonso's religion,
   the heavens will be my witness.
   I believe in Alfonso's Christ, I adore Alfonso's Christ.

BELTRÁN: Better late than never.

ILLÁN: Let's kill her sister too!

SIBILA: Me too? Whatever for?

ILLÁN: To make this scene of vengeance
   more dramatic still.

BELTRÁN: They lie dead on her bed of pleasure.
   And who are you?

BELARDO: I'm the gardener, sir,
   and I happened to be in the garden.

BELTRÁN: He has to die as well.

BELARDO: That's very true, we all have to some day;
   but don't you think it's a bit early for me yet?

BELTRÁN: No-one in this house of evil
   is going to be spared the sword.

BELARDO: I've got something to tell you.

BELTRÁN: What?

BELARDO: Listen.

BELTRÁN: Make it short.

BELARDO: I know where the Jews keep their treasure:
   silver, jewelry, bracelets, that sort of thing.

BELTRÁN: Don't kill him.

ILLÁN: Alright, we'll stop.
   We'll go wherever he wants to take us.

BELARDO: If you could come this way, gentlemen.

BELTRÁN: Let's go.

BELARDO: (*Aside.*) If I give them the slip
   when we've passed the door,
   not even the Cid on his flying horse
   would be able to catch me up.
   (*Exit all, enter ALFONSO and GARCERÁN.*)

ALFONSO: What are you telling me, Manrique?

GARCERÁN: Sire, try and keep your royal dignity,
   don't allow your personal grief to deprive Castile
   of a great king whose deeds have amazed the world.

ALFONSO: But is she dead yet? That's all that interests me.

GARCERÁN: Sire, use your reason. Don't torture yourself
    with the thought that she's still alive.
    I left them all at the door; you surely can't think
    that they stayed outside, and refrained from
    plunging their swords in her white body.
ALFONSO: Then bring me my horses!
GARCERÁN: You've already asked for them,
    they're on their way.
ALFONSO: This reckless fire inside me
    is burning at my entrails!
    I want no-one in my household to survive!
    (*Enter Queen LEONOR and her son, Prince ENRIQUE.*)
LEONOR: Enrique, you better go first.
ENRIQUE: If you want, madam,
    but I'm trembling as well.
ALFONSO: What do you think you're doing?
    How dare you turn up here!
LEONOR: I don't come here as your wife,
    but as the mother of your child,
    whom I want to use in my defence.
    I'm only the frame adorning the
    portrait which you see in front of you;
    if you recognise yourself in this,
    then think of me as just a part of it.
    When a man looks at his son,
    he remembers when he too was young,
    and firm and constant in his ways.
    Look at this, my dear Alfonso, this.
    Look at this precious stone before you,
    not at me, sire, I'm just the mine
    where this shining jewel was found.
    My own life means nothing to me;
    if you are Brutus, then I am Portia;
    but do not throw away this fruit
    even though you burn its branch.
    I don't know why you look so shocked
    on seeing me offer you this hostage;
    you must try and picture me as a cage

in which a small, sweet bird is singing.
Can't you see how much I adore you
and that the more you harm me
the more I love you still.
Surely isn't it time to make our peace
now that our son stands as a judge between us.

ALFONSO: I don't know how you have the nerve
to show your face here.

ENRIQUE: Father, don't be angry.

ALFONSO: What? You've got something to say too?

ENRIQUE: Father, you brought me into this world
so that I could replace you if you had to leave it.
Since God has created me as another you –
you only have to look at us today to see this –
why is it, given now that you are dead,
that I cannot speak on your behalf?

ALFONSO: So, I'm dead, am I?

ENRIQUE: You have been dead for the past seven years:
to be alive is to take control, and not to
leave one's life in the hands of others.
Your duty is to serve Castile, and
you have lost her; you live and yet you do not see –
do you call this living?

ALFONSO: My horses!

GARCERÁN: They're already at the gate sire,
but it's dark already.

ALFONSO: Garcerán, I've gone beyond all fear.
Let the two of us ride to Illescas –
I only hope I'm dead before we're there.

GARCERÁN: How can you be so blinded by the error of
your ways?

ALFONSO: I'm praying to God to shine His torch before me.
(*Exit the King and GARCERÁN.*)

ENRIQUE: Mother, should we not go after him?

LEONOR: Quiet now, there are people coming.
(*Enter BLASCO, BELTRÁN and ILLÁN.*)

BLASCO: Most excellent Queen,
Rachel is lying dead in her room.

LEONOR: And the King? Does he know all the details?

ILLÁN: We agreed that Garcerán should tell him
down in the fields.

LEONOR: Now that Rachel is dead,
this country will be at peace.

BELTRÁN: What's the King been doing?

LEONOR: Terrible things,
he's already ridden off to Madrid.

BLASCO: There are two tasks
I urge you to do:
the first is to follow him;
the second is to speak to him.

LEONOR: These aren't tasks to be taken lightly.
I'm frightened to go. Don't say anything more.

ILLÁN: My lady, Rachel has just died,
and the King must mourn her.
You who love him will have a struggle,
but love always wins in the end.
Speak to the King, bring him your son,
renew your efforts to win him back.

LEONOR: I'm glad you didn't hear
all the things he told me.

ILLÁN: He's still in shock, my lady,
you mustn't let that deter you.

LEONOR: And when should I go?

ILLÁN: Soon.

BLASCO: Now.

LEONOR: I'd better wait till morning.

BLASCO: You must be with him before
the dawn has broken.
Pluck up your courage and go.

ENRIQUE: I want you to go as well,
I'm dying to accompany you.

LEONOR: Let's go then.

ENRIQUE: If he turns violent when he sees you,
let me be your shield again,
and take the full fury of his sword.
(*Exit all, enter King ALFONSO and GARCERÁN.*)

GARCERÁN: So you've no intention of resting on the
journey,
    you've no wish to sleep, sire, not even for a moment?
ALFONSO: How can I sleep off my raging passion?
GARCERÁN: The night is nearly over, and the stars have
begun to fade,
    the horizon is streaked by a band of pure, clear light.
    Morning is breaking with cheeks flushed with pink,
    as if it almost was ashamed to see you in your present state.
ALFONSO: Look, Garcerán, there s no point in talking to
    an obstinate man who knows he's in the right.
    I have every reason to cry.
GARCERÁN: I'm not saying you haven't, but...
ALFONSO: Just go away and have a little sleep.
GARCERÁN: ...why not forget your cares for a while?
ALFONSO: My cares can look after themselves, thank you.
    Just leave me, you're becoming tiresome.
GARCERÁN: I'll be off then.
ALFONSO: Come back when it's a little lighter.
GARCERÁN: I'll do anything you wish, sire.
    (*Exit GARCERÁN.*)
ALFONSO: Your face, Rachel, is lovelier than the dawn sky;
    I am praying for it to watch over me until I die,
    which will be soon. I feel you so close that I see you
    listening to my words and wondering what I'm going to do.
    Be patient, and you'll see me as the reaper with his scythe,
    hacking down your killers until not one of them remains
alive.
    Oh Lord! I'm going crazy as I dwell on my ill fate,
    please rescue me from madness before it is too late!
    I now see Rachel being torn apart and shouting out my
name,
    as if it were me, her lover, who was the one to blame.
    I must act quick, and exact my cruel revenge on every
man.
    Pompous Blasco will be the first to die, and then Illán,
    whose screams on dying will be worse than those of hell;
    Beltrán will be next – I'll consign him to the flames as well.

Even my faithful Garcerán might suffer some violent blow.
There's no knowing how far in my madness I'll be forced
to go.
Watch over me, beautiful Rachel in your rosy cloak of
dawn,
without you here besides me I feel empty, bitter and
forlorn.
Take me from this earth, leave your celestial door ajar –
all that I desire of heaven is to be wherever you are.
What's that light? Are you Rachel? Wait for me!
(*To the sound of music an ANGEL appears suspended from a
pulley.*)

ANGEL: Alfonso, God is greatly offended
by your words, your blasphemies,
your swearing of revenge.
Be yourself once more, unless you take back
what you have said and planned to do,
a terrible punishment will be awaiting you.
God's displeasure is so great that
he is ready to terminate your kingship:
he'll make sure that no child of yours
will ever reach the throne,
but will die instead disgraced and landless.
Be yourself once more, do not say things
that are capable of shocking the stones,
let alone the Heavens, to whose glory
you are eternally in debt.
(*Exit.*)

ALFONSO: I sinned, my Lord; I offended
your Majesty: forgive me.
(*Enter GARCERÁN.*)

GARCERÁN: What in God's name is going on?
Is the King speaking?

ALFONSO: What a terrible sinner I've been!

GARCERÁN: Sire, what are you doing on your knees?

ALFONSO: Why are you so surprised?
Shouldn't a king be on his knees
before an emissary from God?

GARCERÁN: I saw this strange light on entering
    the room; it's fading now.
ALFONSO: That's because I'm absorbing it,
    and emerging at last from the darkness.
    Isn't there a famous
    statue of the Virgin nearby?
GARCERÁN: You must mean the Virgin of Charity.
ALFONSO: Garcerán, I want you to take me there.
GARCERÁN: Sire, I find you changed:
    what's happened to you?
ALFONSO: The same that happened to St Paul
    when he fell off his horse.
    (*Exit, enter the Queen and ENRIQUE, with BLASCO,*
    ILLÁN, BELTRÁN and CLARA, the lady-in-waiting.)
LEONOR: They say he's in here; that he hasn't left yet.
ILLÁN: This is a good place to speak with him.
LEONOR: I must speak first of all to God.
BLASCO: That is always a sound and wise decision.
LEONOR: I feel it's a lucky sign that
    we are in the same building as
    the famous Virgin of Charity,
    whose beauty is said faithfully to reflect
    that of the Queen of Heaven herself.
    I imagine her chapel's the one over there,
    protected by those gilded railings.
    Let's go inside it.
ENRIQUE: May my father's heart be moved today
    by this holiest of Virgins.
LEONOR: If I can achieve peace between us,
    I promise that I'll have this chapel
    sumptuously redecorated from floor to ceiling.
BELTRÁN: We'll rename the place the Chapel of Peace
BLASCO: And isn't peace the greatest
    gift that Charity can give?
    (*They open the shutters that shield the Virgin; the Queen*
    falls to her knees.)
LEONOR: I'm going off to pray, Blasco,
    in that dark corner over there.
BLASCO: Let's leave her on her own, gentlemen.

ILLÁN: Does this place of so many miracles
   have only a single lamp?
BELTRÁN: All the alms that this sanctuary receives
   go towards helping the poor and sick
   and supporting unfortunate widows.
ILLÁN: What a worthy Virgin this is!
BLASCO: And one with a notable history behind her.
BELTRÁN: How did she come to be here?
BLASCO: St Ildefonsus, our great patron of Toledo,
   received this from the Holy Queen herself,
   whom he had pleased with a long poem in her praise.
   This celestial gift was kept at first
   in the saint's private chapel,
   but was later given by him to two devout women,
   whose dedication to the Church and to holy works
   deserved the highest form of recognition.
   It was they who founded this hospital and sanctuary,
   which has grown over the centuries to its present size.
   (*Enter King ALFONSO and GARCERÁN, hurriedly.*)
ALFONSO: Let's get in there quickly,
   I'm withering from too much emotion.
GARCERÁN: The shutters have been opened,
   the Virgin stands before us.
ALFONSO: There's the fountain that will revive
   my sinful, burnt-out soul.
   It's dark in here, so much the better.
   I want to shout my sins aloud.
GARCERÁN: God will hear you even if you're silent.
ALFONSO: I know that, my dear Garcerán.
GARCERÁN: Beg for forgiveness.
ALFONSO: I'll try my best.
   Holy Mary, Mother of God...
LEONOR: You know too well...
ALFONSO: My sins...
LEONOR: How much I depend on you.
ALFONSO: Forgive them.
LEONOR: And that being so...
ALFONSO: May your love...
LEONOR: May my beloved Alfonso...

ALFONSO: Guide me.

LEONOR: Forgive me.

ALFONSO: For you are like a star…

LEONOR: Shine on him…

ALFONSO: And on my Leonor…

LEONOR: So that the love we once shared…

ALFONSO: Returns to save my soul…

LEONOR: And cure him of his illness.

ALFONSO: Garcerán!

GARCERÁN: Sire, what's the matter?

ALFONSO: Could you go and tell that person
over there to pray a bit more quietly.
Her sighs are getting on my nerves.
(*GARCERÁN goes up to the Queen, who is praying with her
face covered.*)

GARCERÁN: Please, don't stop your prayers.
But there's a gentleman across the aisle
who's in a rather emotional state
and would be grateful if your devotions
did not compete so much with his.
He's had a bad shock recently,
and his nerves are on edge.
The slightest noise
drives him almost to distraction.

LEONOR: Tell the gentleman that his sufferings
could not be greater than mine.
I've lost a husband whose
virtues stand comparison with no-one,
bar Alfonso VIII;
but I'll lower my voice,
if he wants me to.

GARCERÁN: I'll tell him to respect your grief.
(*He returns to the King.*)

LEONOR: Wasn't that Garcerán?

ENRIQUE: It seemed like him.
Does that mean that my dear father is here as well?

LEONOR: It does indeed.
I entreat you once again, sweet Virgin,
to reconcile me with my husband.

ALFONSO: Then let her cry, if she needs to.
    Perhaps her tears might help
    to soften further my hardened heart.
    (*CLARA speaks to GARCERÁN while kneeling down beside him.*)
CLARA: Garcerán! It's me!
GARCERÁN: That's a lovely and familiar voice.
    It's the beautiful Clara!
CLARA: Do you know who you were just talking to?
    The Queen.
GARCERÁN: Good God! And do you realise
    that the sighing man is the King?
    You'll find him all changed.
    I'll be back in a moment.
    Sire, the Queen…
ALFONSO: Is weeping for all the harm that has been done
                                    her…
GARCERÁN: Is here.
ALFONSO: And she has every right to.
LEONOR: (*To CLARA.*) When he got up like that,
    I began to think he wasn't Garcerán after all.
CLARA: The King, he told me, is a changed person.
    He's ready to throw himself in your arms.
    Don't you see how repentant he is?
LEONOR: I certainly do. That must be God's influence.
    I must talk to him now.
ALFONSO: (*To GARCERÁN.*) I was deep in prayer, Garcerán,
    I didn't take in at first the wonderful
    news you've brought me.
ENRIQUE: Let's hope that God really has softened his heart.
LEONOR: I'm putting my trust in Him.
ALFONSO: My darling Queen, my only true companion!
    Have you finished voicing your grief
    and begging God for us to be reconciled?
    Garcerán, have you ever heard such heart-felt sighs?
    Those were sighs equal to the pain caused by
    a man who has loved another and forgotten his kingdom.
    All I can do now is to throw myself at your feet,

and hope that God accepts my humble gesture
and grants a peaceful conclusion to all this misery.
(*While saying this, the King walks up to the trembling Queen.*)
LEONOR: Oh Jesus!
ALFONSO: Don't be frightened, it's me, the Alfonso you
                       knew before.
I swear before the Virgin of Charity that I've been blind
these past seven years; I entreat the Virgin to guard my
                       sight
from now onwards, and to make sure I have eyes only
                       for my
beautiful Leonor, whom I shall adore until the end of my
                       days,
until I have fully repaid all that I owe her.
(*They embrace.*)
LEONOR: I am unworthy of these embraces.
GARCERÁN: Come here, all of you.
BELTRÁN: Who are these people? Clear off.
GARCERÁN: It's the King.
BLASCO: Sire!
ALFONSO: Friends, I know now that I lost my way.
Try and forget the errors of my past.
ILLÁN: Well spoken.
ENRIQUE: My dear father,
now that you aren't so angry,
can I hold your hand?
ALFONSO: You can have my arms as well.
Let's go back to Toledo,
where we'll celebrate our reunion
with a thousand festivities.
BLASCO: We'll make them the finest
that the city has ever seen.
ILLÁN: And on this note of peace and reconciliation
we end our story of love and loyalties
and blindness dispelled by faith –
the true story of Alfonso VIII.

The End.

THE INNOCENT CHILD

Characters

QUEEN ISABEL

KING FERDINAND

DON IÑIGO DE MENDOZA

DOÑA JUANA

SAINT DOMINIC

BENITO GARCÍA (DE LAS MESURAS), a Jew

FRANCISCO, a Jew

OCAÑA, a Jew

HERNANDO, a Jew

QUINTANAR

PEDRO DE LA GUARDIA

RABBI

JACOB, a Jew

BERNARDO, a Frenchman

ROSELA, his wife

PASAMONTES

JUANA GUINDERA, his wife

JUANICO, their son

BLAS, a swineheard

TURÓN, a swineheard

TEACHER

BOYS

TWO ANGELS

MILLER

MILLER'S WIFE

REASON

INTELLECT

HERRERA, an officer of the Inquisition

MARÍA, his wife

MUSICIANS

DOCTOR

BLIND WOMAN

This translation of *The Innocent Child* was commissioned by Globe Education and first performed in a staged reading by Stranger's Gallery at the Globe Education Centre Theatre, London, on 21 June 1998, with the following cast:

ISABEL/MILLER'S WIFE/REASON, Carolyn Backhouse

FERDINAND/BERNARDO/INTELLECT/ HERRERA, Simon Coury

IÑIGO/TEACHER/TURÕN, Matthew Mills

DOÑA JUANA/ROSELA/MARÎA, Clare Burt

DOMINIC/RABBI/DOCTOR, Mike Burnside

BENITO, Paul Virag

FRANCISCO, Peter Forbes

OCAÑA/JACOB, David Terence

HERNANDO, Larry Lamb

QUINTANAR, Jack Klaff

PEDRO/BLAS, Issac Maxwell-Hunt

PASAMONTES/MILLER, Simon Harvey

JUANA, Joanne Howarth

JUANICO, Ben Hayward

ANGEL/BLIND WOMAN, Valerie Sarruf

Other parts played by members of the Company

Co-ordinator, Colin Ellwood

ACT ONE

Enter Queen ISABEL, DON IÑIGO DE MENDOZA, and DOÑA JUANA, a lady-in-waiting.

ISABEL: And where is my Lord the King?

IÑIGO: With our holy father Torquemada.
    They are deep in conversation.

ISABEL: His dedication to the cause
    never ceases to astonish me!

IÑIGO: I have never seen His Majesty
    quite like this before.
    Mind you, in matters of the Faith,
    He has always been vigilant,
    especially in dealing with heresy,
    which is like a poisonous snake
    slithering towards his feet.

ISABEL: Iñigo, this vile serpent that
    continues to breed in our land
    will be crushed into the ground
    by the weight of the Holy Inquisition.
    I hope for the sake of God
    that this noble institution,
    which we shall bring to Castile,
    will defend the faith with
    such strength and conviction
    that the yolk which is our emblem
    will rise above this heretical pollution
    and reinforce its hold over all of Spain.

IÑIGO: Your zeal is an example to us all.

ISABEL: Our religion will never be pure
    as long as it is stained
    by this cankerous heresy.

IÑIGO: What will become of our race
    if the various bloods continue
    so freely to mingle together?

ISABEL: A spotted, stunted offspring
    – that's what happens when you couple

a pure white mare with a black nag.
The Spanish race has put up too long
with these lowliest of curs.
They drag us down to their muddy level
to besmirch the purity of our blood.

IÑIGO: May your virtue grow with the King's
and that of our divine Inquisition
so that Spain will be cleansed of its impurities.

ISABEL: Go, Marquis of Santillana,
and tell us if there is any more news.

IÑIGO: May the Lord protect you.

(*Exit.*)

ISABEL: Doña Juana!

DOÑA JUANA: My lady?

ISABEL: That wonderful young man,
that shining example of Castillian valour,
has renewed my hopes for Spain.

DOÑA JUANA: For his deeds both in peace and in war,
Don Iñigo has been called the Spanish phoenix.

ISABEL: Have you brought my *Book of Hours*?

DOÑA JUANA: I have it here, my lady.

ISABEL: Give it to me, I want to read it.

DOÑA JUANA: But I thought you had to do some writing.

ISABEL: Later yes, but not now.
For the moment I wish to pray for a while.

DOÑA JUANA: In her piety she is like a shining sun!
She brings glory to the Church and to the Crown.

(*Exit, the Queen is left sitting on a cushion, holding her Book of Hours.*)

ISABEL: No sooner do my eyes touch the page
than I can hardly keep them open.
The greatest gift in life would be
to overcome these mortal failings.
Please, sleep, let me read,
I need always to be alert
if I am going to rule my country.
Oh, the endless cares of the throne.
and even more so for a woman!

Perhaps I should let my Ferdinand do everything,
he is so much cleverer and more virtuous,
and yet I know he wants me always by his side.
But why does sleep want to come now,
of all times? Alright then, I give in,
I cannot fight you any longer,
there is no point in holding back
a force as strong as sleep.
*(To the sound of flageolets a curtain opens, and SAINT
DOMINIC appears with his traditional emblems – a spray
of white lilies in his hand, and a dog at his feet bearing a
lighted torch.)*
DOMINIC: Most enlightened Isabel,
noble and pure-blooded descendant
of the Castillian Kings
and the Spanish Goths,
I am Dominic, and share with you,
not only your land and country,
but also your very blood,
for I too am from the House of Castile.
You will have heard much about me
from learned men; but the part of my story
that has meant most to our family,
has been my zealous support of the Faith
and my battle against heresy.
When my mother prayed to have a son
she dreamt, Isabel, of this symbol you see
of my zeal – the dog with the flaming torch.
The dog's barkings are the many sermons
I gave all over Spain, Italy and France;
the torch is the fire which I,
like another Samson, wielded in my campaigns
against Christ's vilifiers.
For I was the very first Inquisitor,
and the order I founded carried out
the work of the Holy Office with such fervour
that when our Peter Martyr was killed by heretics
the blood that poured from his head wound

fell on the ground to form the word 'Credo'.
The number of my men martyred
by the sword, burnt at the stake,
hung on the gallows, pierced by lances,
and stoned to death, is too long to list;
but it goes without saying that their memories,
like pictures in a gallery,
have been placed in the heavens,
adorned with a thousand palms and laurels.
Yours and Ferdinand's worthy intentions
in bringing back our holy Inquisition,
and defending its causes by tribunal,
have pleased God so greatly
that you can be assured not only
of the greatest reward in heaven,
but also of long life, triumphs,
glories, an expanding empire,
a line of distinguished descendants
from the noble House of Austria.
Charles V, your grandson, will curtail
the Protestant scourge by exiling Luther
from his lands; Philip II will emulate his
good deeds, as will his son, Philip III, and
his two daughters, the Infantas Ana and María.
But first, of all, great Isabel,
you must know that the Inquisition,
however hard it tries, cannot on its own
expel for ever the Jews from Spain.
You too must act, and prepare an edict
ordering their immediate departure,
so that this country should be cleansed
once and for all of their dark infamy.

ISABEL: Please wait, holy Dominic!
Jesus! What a clear vision is this!
I cannot believe it is just a dream.
Don't go, father, don't go!
(*Enter the King.*)

FERDINAND: What is happening, my lady?
Who are you speaking to?

ISABEL: I must have been dreaming,
    but I'm not sure. I seem
    to have been talking in my sleep.
    I had just sat down here to pray
    when I was suddenly overcome by sleep.
    Has Brother Torquemada gone yet?
FERDINAND: Yes, my lady.
ISABEL: What were you talking about?
FERDINAND: The Papal Bull, it has just arrived.
    Our every wish has been granted.
    We have now the blessing of the Pope to
    found here, in Castile, the holy Inquisition,
    The glory of the Faith is now assured,
    I have already begun to appoint its officers.
ISABEL: This is great news indeed, dear Ferdinand,
    but do not think that the mere
    sanctioning of this institution
    is enough to rid us of our worries.
    We must go further – we must cut off the head
    of this impious serpent in our midst.
FERDINAND: Isabel, let me remind you of Hercules,
    the Greek hero whose labours
    earned him happiness and fame.
    When he fought with the Lernaean Hydra,
    he too had to cut off a monster's head.
    But no sooner had one head fallen,
    than seven more had risen in its place,
    each one uglier and more horrid than before.
    Eventually, as his stubborn enemy persisted,
    he found a way to stop the monster's growth
    by placing a hot flame at the point
    where the neck had just been severed.
    In this he was assisted by a friend,
    who wielded the fiery brand while Hercules
    set about the head with club and steel.
    I am like Hercules, cutting off
    heresy at the neck, while my friend the Inquisition –
    my inseparable companion who will

help me to spread the glory of our faith –
is the one who will have to place the flame.

ISABEL: I have no doubt, Ferdinand,
that everyone will soon be calling you
another Hercules, if that is what you want.
But all that interests me now is how
to deal with these pestilential Jews.
Let us throw them out of Spain,
let us make them strangers in a foreign land.
They can go to Africa; they can live in Asia.
But they cannot stay here in our land,
for they are a noxious and obstinate race.
If faith is like the sun, then they are
the clouds who wish to eclipse it.
For Christ's sake, Ferdinand,
it is us who must put a stop to this,
for we are the pillars of the Faith.
We must send them this instant to a faraway
place where their evil gaze will not reach us!
They are worse than snakes,
they are basilisks...
Enough said.

FERDINAND: My pious queen, my concerns
are the same as yours,
as the heavens know only too well.

ISABEL: If only I could tell you
what I saw in my dreams.

FERDINAND: The heavens too have directed me
in dreams to banish the Jews.

ISABEL: The person who delays in carrying out this
command seems to me a person of little faith.
Sire, you must prepare an edict ordering
every one of them to go.

FERDINAND: Yes, I shall do so, and,
just to show you
how strong is my faith,
I shall have it written out today.

ISABEL: And make sure they bring
all their belongings and families.

FERDINAND: You can see you are a fervent
    guardian of the Faith.
    I hope soon to show you
    how much I value your fervour.
ISABEL: You have always been my inspiration,
    all my virtue I have got from you.
FERDINAND: But kings can only be virtuous
    if they follow the laws of God
    the King, the maker of all kings.
    (*Exit, and enter the Jews BENITO GARCÍA, HERNANDO,
    and FRANCISCO.*)
HERNANDO: What bitter words can express the bitterness
                            I feel,
    or live up to the sadness you see written on my face?
    I shall die of anger, if I don't give in before to grief!
BENITO: Ever since that sad and painful day, Hernando,
    when I discovered what was meant by Christ's tribunal.
    I have lost all will to live, and gladly await my death.
    What sort of monarchs are these who dream up
    all these charges against poor, harmless people
    who keep to themselves, and to their own private beliefs?
    What fire is this that, after being dead for so long,
    is suddenly rekindled by whole armies of Dominicans?
    What is this new black and white Cross
    that brings so much joy to the Catholics?
    What are all these new laws and investigations?
    What are all these secrets that are being uncovered?
FRANCISCO: What sad, unfortunates we are, we who have
                           barely known
    happiness in all our centuries of rootless wanderings!
    All that misery which was foretold for us so long ago
    shows no sign of ending, we are being punished still.
HERNANDO: Our lives are worthless, all we have left is
                          despair
    while we await the cruel conclusion to our tragic fate.
    Oh Great Lord! How much more time have we to wait
    before you send the Messiah to redeem us?
    We have lost our empire and all our priests,

Nebuchadnezzah destroyed our most holy of temples,
and the famous Porch of Solomon lies in ruins,
its ivory throne choked in useless ivy,
and its once mighty walls now barely two stones high.
What miserable beings are we Spanish Jews,
stranded at sea without a single port in sight!
Already a new Inquisition is baying for our blood,
anxious to expose our every so-called secret.
We, who thought that no-one would bark at us
once Dominic's black dog was dead, have since found
ourselves being chased by the whole bloody kennel.

BENITO: Remember, Hernando, those two inquisitors of old,
Brother Eymeric and Cardinal Roselli, whose zeal was
such as to destroy the greatest and wealthiest
of our race in Aragón and Catalonia. But all their power
came to nothing once their two henchmen, Ponce and
Ladireta,
had been killed by the irate mob, with stones and poison.
And thus I hope that our oppressed people in Castile
will soon exact their furtive vengeance, and make war
against the enemy even though their swords be sheathed.

FRANCISCO: But how can we possibly kill them?

BENITO: In France there is a rabbi who is also
the most famous sorcerer we have at present.
He will find a way.

HERNANDO: Then it's up to us to go and find him.

FRANCISCO: And to do so as soon as possible,
for time is short, Benito.

BENITO: Our very lives are at stake,
I shall set off immediately.

HERNANDO: Bring back his sorcery, and make sure it does
away with all those inquisitors and officials
who have been causing us all our recent troubles.

FRANCISCO: We'll see how far their pure blood gets them!
They might think of themselves as Caesars,
but they'll end up no better off than the Moors.

BENITO: Praise be to the God of David, whom I adore!
(*Exit BENITO.*)

HERNANDO: May He who saved Elijah from Jezebel,
    who came to Daniel in the lion's den,
    who protected Zacharias from Nabuc,
    who prolonged the life of Ezechiel,
    and who freed Judith from the wrath
    of the savage army of Holofernes,
    May He guide you on your mission.

FRANCISCO: These evil bastards won't escape this time!

HERNANDO: Not a single inquisitor will be spared!

FRANCISCO: Let the Christian barbarians perish,
    let them all die from mysterious wounds!

HERNANDO: Even though we go unarmed we shall avenge
    ourselves in ways they shall never forget.
    And even if they attack us with wild elephants,
    we shall fight back as bravely as the Maccabeans.

FRANCISCO: Who are those people coming towards us?

HERNANDO: Don't worry, it's only Pedro de la Guardia,
    accompanied by some musicians.
    (*Enter PEDRO and the MUSICIANS.*)

PEDRO: What's up, my friends?

HERNANDO: Oh Pedro, you won't believe what's happening.
    It's what you've always prayed for – we're finally
    going to have our vengeance on the Christians.

PEDRO: What's this you're telling me?

HERNANDO: Benito…

PEDRO: You mean García de las Mesuras?

HERNANDO: That's the one. He's gone off to France.

PEDRO: To France? Whatever for?

HERNANDO: To seek out this rabbi whose secret powers
    we hope will kill off all the Christians,
    or at the very least every Dominican friar.

PEDRO: Oh great God of Jacob, it seems that this great
    day will coincide with the arrival of the Messiah,
    which had been so long promised to our forefathers!
    Today I was with a friend who had been told in confidence
    that the Messiah, through fear of the Christian dogs,
    would be arriving by way of the Tagus, disguised as a fish.

FRANCISCO: Heavens above!
    This is extraordinary news indeed!

PEDRO: I was just telling you what he said.

HERNANDO: But can't you see that this contradicts
what is written down in our scriptures,
which insist that he will be a man of virgin born?

FRANCISCO: It's best not to get involved in matters that
would appear to support the faith of the Christians,
who believe that Christ has already visited us and that
his mother was a virgin before, during and after the birth.

PEDRO: That's enough of all this theology.
It's time we heard these musicians,
who have come here to sing you a psalm.

A MUSICIAN: We are ready.

PEDRO: Well go on and sing then,
and let the music express our sorrows.
(*The MUSICIANS sing.*)

MUSICIANS:
'Oh God, the heathen
have come into your land,
and defiled the holy temple,
and laid Jerusalem to waste.
The dead bodies of your
servants have been left as
food for birds and beasts.
Their pure blood has flowed;
but no-one could bury them.
Already we have been mocked
and scorned by our neighbours.
When, oh Lord, will be worthy
enough for you to forgive us?
Let your anger now be turned
against our persecutors and
not against those who adore you!'
(*Enter QUINTANAR.*)

QUINTANAR: Why do you resort to plaintive song
when you should be screaming out to the heavens,
ill-fated Jews, condemned for ever
to live without a homeland?
Why bother with gentle harmonies
and softly plucked lyres when

you are no better off than
the slaves of Babylon, forced
to sing by cruel masters?
Now that you are captives in Spain,
why not ask, as the Babylonians did,
'How can we sing in a strange land?'

HERNANDO: 'If I forget thee, Oh Jerusalem, let my
tongue cleave to the roof of my mouth!'
But come on, Quintanar, tell us the worst.
What more bad news are you bringing us?
What's happening in Toledo?
Have any more of those black and white
Dominican dogs been sent out to get us?
Are they just barking, or are they now biting?
Have they got some other *Auto da Fe* planned?
Have they got the old fire burning again?
How many more poor souls are in for a good grilling?
What new little statute have they tagged on to the Papal
Bull?

QUINTANAR: Isabel and Fernando have ordered
all of their unbaptised subjects
to leave immediately their kingdom.
In obeyance of this sad order,
shouted out by criers throughout the land,
over two hundred families have
already embarked on the path of exile.
What painful sights are to be seen –
old men supported by their grandchildren;
husbands, with silent shameful faces,
looking after luggage and servants,
and consoling weeping wives;
beautiful young women, with their
hair loose and flowing in the air,
still capable of breaking passing hearts.
Have you ever seen pictures of Aeneas
fleeing Troy to escape the fury of the Greeks,
his old father clinging to his back,
his wife trailing sadly behind them,
and their son gripping his hand?

Well, now you can imagine the Jews
in their exodus from Spain,
their lands sold off cheaply,
their furniture all destroyed,
their houses pulled to the ground.
And I cannot help feeling that
this sorry story will not end here,
and that Isabel will not be happy
until she has destroyed us all.

HERNANDO: If only the Castillian throne
was in Portugese hands,
if only Ferdinand and Isabel
were dead, then we would have
lost our greatest enemy!
Now all our hope lies in Benito,
who has gone off to France
in search of a sorcerer.

QUINTANAR: You've put your faith in sorcery?

FRANCISCO: There's a famous French Rabbi
who is an expert in these matters.
He'll help us kill off
all these barking Dominicans.

PEDRO: What on earth has got over Isabel?
Doesn't she know that wealthy Jews
were once the favourites of the Spanish kings?

QUINTANAR: Pedro, let's get going,
I hear hostile voices.

HERNANDO: Look out!

FRANCISCO: Shhh!

PEDRO: Quiet!

(*Exit the Jews, enter PASAMONTES and JUANICO, holding
a book.*)

PASAMONTES: You'll be much better off, Juan,
in this new school; it's nearer home,
you won't suffer so much from the sun,
and it's even a good place for the winter,
especially for someone so young and delicate.
Did your mother give you a good breakfast?

JUANICO: She did, sir.

PASAMONTES: You know, you're a lucky boy.
　　God, your true father,
　　must have taken a shine to you.
　　Did you say your prayers, this morning?

JUANICO: Yes sir, all four of them.

PASAMONTES: Pay attention to the words,
　　and always say them with good grace.
　　You must never have
　　anything else on your mind
　　when you're praying. Do you hear me?

JUANICO: Yes sir.

PASAMONTES: The teacher is a good Christian,
　　and always punctual, you must try and
　　be like him. You'll learn in life that
　　time is short, and that if you don't
　　make good use of it, you'll end up
　　an ignoramus, respected by no-one.
　　Never be like that, and make sure
　　instead you know your true worth,
　　which is considerable, for you're
　　the shining image of your mother.
　　Do you understand?

JUANICO: Yes sir.

PASAMONTES: What book did the boy buy you?

JUANICO: The Lives of the Child Saints Justus and Pastor.

PASAMONTES: He couldn't have made a better choice.

JUANICO: Father, I asked for it myself,
　　it's such a lovely story,
　　and it even talks about
　　what they did in school.

PASAMONTES: It's with stories such as these
　　that God reveals his greatness
　　to the children of this world.
　　Read it with loving attention,
　　and you'll find out how cheerfully
　　the two boys went to meet their deaths.
　　If you were threatened with martyrdom
　　would you be so willing to die for God?

JUANICO: I certainly would!
  If only I had the opportunity!
PASAMONTES: But don't you know how cruel death is?
  Doesn't it frighten you in any way?
JUANICO: They say that dying for God
  is a beautiful death.
PASAMONTES: That's very true.
JUANICO: If it was wonderful for those two,
  it will be the same for me, sir.
PASAMONTES: When I look at you,
  I see something almost saint-like,
  I don't know what it is.
  Well, here we are at the school.
  (*Classroom sounds from within.*)
JUANICO: All that shouting is a good sign.
  There must be many pupils here.
PASAMONTES: The teacher has the reputation of
  having the best school in Toledo.
  But what's wrong with you?
  You're not frightened, I hope!
JUANICO: I'm not frightened, sir.
PASAMONTES: Don't worry, lad,
  I'll make sure you'll not get beaten.
JUANICO: But if I've deserved a beating,
  why don't you want me to have one?
  Let them beat me, I've got to learn.
  (*Enter the TEACHER with two or three PUPILS; he is
  wearing a gown and cutting a pen.*)
TEACHER: Take this pen.
PUPIL: It's, it's a bit too fine for me.
TEACHER: Speak more clearly, boy!
PUPIL: My handwriting is big and rounded...
PASAMONTES: May God protect you.
TEACHER: And you as well.
  (*To the PUPIL.*)
  Look, Leonardo, you're going to
  have to make do with this,
  you've got an exam coming up.
PUPIL: I shall try my best sir.

PASAMONTES: I've brought you my son,
    he wasn't happy at his last school.
TEACHER: Come here, my boy, don't be shy.
    What are you reading?
JUANICO: I'm reading a book.
TEACHER: The cheeky rascal!
PASAMONTES: It's only his nerves.
TEACHER: I'll soon teach him some manners.
    Well come on then, read us out a bit.
    I want to find out how much you've learnt.
PASAMONTES: This is going to be interesting,
    we only bought him the book this morning.
JUANICO: "And when Justus, most blessed among
    children, saw how his martyrdom would be used by the
    evil tyrant to try and frighten his brother Pastor out of
    his faith, he turned his divine and radiant face towards
    him and said: 'Pastor, do not be afraid of death, and do
    not think of it as an injustice for innocents like ourselves,
    for though we are children, Christ was more innocent
    than us'".
TEACHER: You don't have to read any more.
    You have already overtaken the whole class.
PASAMONTES: He's quite an intelligent boy.
TEACHER: He certainly has promise,
    I'll be happy to take him on,
    and become his second father.
    Trust me.
PASAMONTES: I can't pay you just yet.
TEACHER: You don't owe me anything so far.
PASAMONTES: Come back home, Juan,
    to collect your things.
JUANICO: I shall do so, sir.
TEACHER: And bring me the money when you return.
    Don't come here this afternoon without it.
JUANICO: I shall bring it.
TEACHER: Do you know how to pray?
JUANICO: Of course, I do.
TEACHER: You'll remember the money?

JUANICO: Yes.

TEACHER: May God protect you.
    (*They leave, enter BENITO, the RABBI, and JACOB.*)

BENITO: I swear by the God of the Great David,
    that you have won me over, Rabbi,
    with this magical plan of yours.

RABBI: It's absolutely infallible, believe me.

JACOB: I'm sure you're right,
    but where are we going to find
    this heart of a Christian child,
    let alone the wafer from a Christian altar?

RABBI: The holy wafer won't be a problem.
    I know an old woman who's easy to bribe –
    we'll trick her into taking
    one and keeping it safely.
    As for getting the child whose heart
    you must remove – and this is
    essential for the magic to work,
    for the heart and the host must be
    mixed together before being able
    to poison the waters of any river –
    I have in mind this nobleman
    who has fallen on such hard times
    that he'll even give away one of his
    ten children if we give him enough money.

JACOB: But is there really a Christian
    who would sell off his child?

RABBI: I promise you there is.

JACOB: And I promise you he must be bloody mad.

RABBI: That's only because you're rich,
    and can supply the money
    that he would kill to have.
    Have you not read in the Bible
    about those children who were
    so hungry in wartime that
    they had to eat their mothers?

JACOB: Do you mean that time when our holy city
    was being besieged by the Romans?

RABBI: Yes. Well if hunger made that happen
    in Jerusalem, it would surely have
    the same effect in France as well.

BENITO: I agree with you completely.
    And if Jacob does not want to help
    I shall buy the child myself
    with the money I have been given
    by those who sent me here from Spain.
    I have no intention of going home
    before seeing the sorcery carried out.

JACOB: If gold is enough inducement
    to sell off one's flesh and blood,
    then I am not as rich as I thought.

BENITO: I like the idea of a child being bought,
    it makes him more like Christ.

RABBI: Be quiet! We've reached the man's house.
    I can hear him walking behind the door.

BENITO: Is that a man?

RABBI: Can't you tell by his step?

BERNARDO: (*From inside.*) Who's that at the door? Who's
                                          there?

RABBI: Friends, Bernardo.

BERNARDO: Who is it?

(*Enter BERNARDO.*)

RABBI: You're looking well, Bernardo.

BERNARDO: Good lord! What are you doing here, Rabbi?

RABBI: Bernardo, although I could give you many reasons
    for my wanting to be with you, I don't want to bore you,
    and, besides, I thought we had a close understanding.
    Think how many times you have come up to my house
    to unburden yourself of all your problems,
    to tell me with tears streaming from your eyes
    about your difficulties in supporting your wife and children.
    By the way, how many have you got?

BERNARDO: Haven't I already told you I had ten?

RABBI: I know that this is a painful subject,
    but how would you feel if one of them should die
    so that the others had a better chance of living?

BERNARDO: If God should take away one of them,
    and find a way of helping the others,
    then that at least would be a certain consolation.
RABBI: Well then, Bernardo, listen to this:
    the three of us here would like to offer one thousand
    ducats if you kill one of them...
BERNARDO: This is preposterous!
RABBI: ...because we need his heart for
    some sacrificial rite called for by our religion.
BERNARDO: God would not permit me, sirs,
    to sell off my flesh and blood for such a purpose.
    If any of them die of hunger or of poverty,
    at least I myself won't be to blame.
    Leave immediately, I would hate my wife
    to hear what we've been talking about.
JACOB: For one thousand ducats you'd have
    no more worries about any of them dying poor.
BERNARDO: I've already told you
    I don't want your blood money!
RABBI: Be quiet! Don't shout!
BERNARDO: May God protect you.
RABBI: We haven't even started to bargain.
BERNARDO: I can't believe that necessity
    has brought matters to this!
    (*The Jews leave, enter ROSELA, the wife of BERNARDO.*)
ROSELA: I've been hiding behind this curtain,
    and have heard everything that's been said.
BERNARDO: Oh, my darling Rosela,
    did you really hear what they were asking for?
ROSELA: Yes.
BERNARDO: One thousand ducats would certainly
    help to solve our problems,
    but is there anyone who would
    sell off his flesh and blood
    even had the sum been two thousand ducats?
ROSELA: What would you say if I told you
    I could make the child appear dead,
    and replace his heart with that of a pig,

which looks very similar?

Wouldn't you call me a clever woman?

BERNARDO: Is it possible to seem dead while staying
alive?

ROSELA: If you're a good enough actor.

BERNARDO: That's true.

ROSELA: The performance would be improved
if I pretend to scorn the money
these vile creatures give you!

BERNARDO: And they're the ones who
think they're being clever!

ROSELA: 'My flesh and blood for this,
you filthy dogs?' How's that?
Come on, Bernardo, go and call them back.

BERNARDO: Shouldn't we first find the sucking pig?

ROSELA: You're right. Unless we can produce a heart,
this will all end in tears.

BERNARDO: There are always pigs being herded
along the nearby river-bank,
but they're very well guarded.

ROSELA: I wouldn't steal one if I were you,
because pigs are noisy beasts,
and you're bound to be caught out.
I've got a much better idea.

BERNARDO: A better one?

ROSELA: Go and buy one, and bring it here,
and say you'll give the money tomorrow.
I hope you'll pay out, for my sake, for
you'll soon be one thousand ducats the richer.

BERNARDO: I'll try and see what I can do.

ROSELA: In the meantime, I'll set about preparing
the other part of the trick.

BERNARDO: Which of our sons are you going to kill?

ROSELA: Clemente will be the best at feigning death.

BERNARDO: Well, I'll be off then,
you seem to know what you're doing.

ROSELA: You're bound to get the thousand ducats.

BERNARDO: If you, as a woman, succeed in tricking such clever
    men as these, you'll deserve a medal, for sure.
    (Exit, enter BLAS and TURÕN, swineherds.)
BLAS: Have they had their drink?
TURÕN: They have indeed.
BLAS: Well let's be going then.
TURÕN: We can't yet, I'm truly pissed off,
    one of the young pigs
    is taking his time in the water,
    he's a right big bugger and all,
    he's almost as big as you.
BLAS: Well pull him hard by the tail!
TURÕN: There's no budging that fellow,
    I can tell you.
BLAS: Let him be then, he just wants a bath.
TURÕN: This is the last fucking straw,
    I've had enough of this,
    I'm going away for good!
BLAS: What's up with you?
TURÕN: I had a few words with the boss yesterday,
    and every time I go and see him
    to ask for the hand of…you know who,
    he tells me to sod off…
BLAS: Well, where do you think you'll go to?
TURÕN: Where? Where I can have a better life than this,
    I don't even want to marry now if he's going
    to be sniffing around her all the time.
BLAS: I imagine the old man's waiting for his wife to die
    so he can marry the young lass himself…
TURÕN: Are you sure?
BLAS: Crispín has seen him trying
    to give her the odd squeeze and cuddle,
    and that doesn't look good to me.
    Turón, you shouldn't worry so much,
    let him become a widower, so he can marry her,
    so that she'll soon be widowed too,
    and then it'll be your turn, as simple as that.

TURÕN: That's bloody typical of you,
    you're always knocking a man when he's down!
    You want me to wait for those two to die
    while I amuse myself with the fucking pigs?
BLAS: Not exactly, let me put it another way:
    isn't it better to grow a flower from a
    cutting than to start off from seed?
TURÕN: Sod your arty metaphors, I'll be more direct:
    do you want me spend every winter
    seeing her nice and cosy in the boss's bed
    while I freeze my balls off on the stone floor?
    (*Enter BERNARDO.*)
BERNARDO: (I shall try and seem confident)
    Hello there, my dear swineherds!
BLAS: Who's that wanker?
BERNARDO: Would you like to sell me a sucking pig?
TURÕN: You want a pig for fucking with?
BERNARDO: All I asked was to buy one, for God's sake!
BLAS: It wouldn't do any harm, Turón to sell him one.
TURÕN: If you want to buy one, it's all yours.
BERNARDO: How much is that one over there?
TURÕN: Oooh, look where he's pointing to!
BERNARDO: Cut the jokes please!
TURÕN: They suck, do they?
    Okay, I'll be serious,
    for you it's worth six ducats.
BERNARDO: Will you give it to me for four?
TURÕN: No fucking way!
BERNARDO: Alright, four and a half, then.
TURÕN: Can't you see how fat and juicy he is?
BERNARDO: In the old days you'd have been ashamed to
                                               sell
    such a thin and miserable creature.
BLAS: Just let him have it,
    we're not the sort of people
    to haggle over the odd ducat or two.
    We're not your common garden swineherds.
TURÕN: Yes, I'm happy for you to have it.

BERNARDO: Phew! That's good to hear.
Well, tie him up then and bring him
to that house over there.
TURÕN: Not so fast, what about the money?
BERNARDO: You'll get it soon, don't worry.
TURÕN: And where are you off to?
BERNARDO: To see some friends.
TURÕN: I'll come with you.
BERNARDO: (Oh no, what bad luck,
may heaven help me!)
(*Exit, enter JACOB, the RABBI, and BENITO.*)
RABBI: Bernardo's come to see me about a child.
JACOB: So he's finally succumbed.
BENITO: When faced with necessity, what other choice is
there
but to renounce one's principles?
JACOB: You should still be careful though, he might be doing
this out of malice, to turn the authorities against us.
RABBI: The authorities? Why should he do that?
What have we done to him?
JACOB: I don't think you understand how Christians
function.
Whenever they find a man who can be of use to them
they stretch out a hand of friendship only to bring him
down.
BENITO: But this is France not Spain. The notaries, the
scribes,
the officers of justice, are all honest here;
they're not insolent, they don't abuse their power
or go against the letter of the law.
They value friendships highly, they are discreet,
well thought of, and have nobility in their souls.
JACOB: But we Jews are among enemies wherever we go:
thus we must always be doubly on our guard,
and assume that nothing that is said is what is meant,
and that no person is the same as what he seems.
RABBI: I think your worries are ill-founded,
for I am an astrologer, and know that

we are dealing with a simple, honest man
who is fearful of Christ's law.
BENITO: Alright, I believe you. But what about the holy
wafer?
RABBI: If I can persuade that old woman,
who lives in the house across the street,
She will take away the wafer in her mouth
and then wrap it up in her hood.
JACOB: Do you think she'll agree to this?
RABBI: That woman would do anything for money –
she'd be as quick to kill her son
as Judas was quick to sell his God!
Come on, let's be going.
JACOB: Let's hope this has a happy ending.
RABBI: You'll soon see the effect of my sorcery,
when hundreds start dying from the
river that we'll contaminate.
BENITO: Show us the way,
for God seems to be lighting up your path.
(*Exit, enter ROSELA and BERNARDO.*)
BERNARDO: Has that bumpkin gone yet?
ROSELA: I managed to trick him into going.
BERNARDO: Well, I've cut open the pig myself,
and placed the bloody heart next to Clemente.
ROSELA: You must have seen what a good job
I did with the child.
I rubbed his face with saffron,
and his neck with blood,
and then ruffled his hair a bit.
The effect was so life-like
that I even fooled myself,
and began to cry when I saw him.
BERNARDO: There's a knock on our door.
Do you think it's them?
ROSELA: I don't know.
Yes it is, they're coming in!
(*Enter the RABBI, JACOB and BENITO.*)
RABBI: May God dwell in this house.

ROSELA: I'm going to tell everyone what you've done,
    I'll shout it out as loud as I can,
    I'm going to say you've killed my darling Clemente,
    my sweet, brown-eyed innocent little boy!
BERNARDO: If you don't lower your voice
    I'm going to use this dagger
    to do the same to you as I did to him!
RABBI: For God's sake Bernardo try and control yourself!
ROSELA: Are you pleased with your thousand ducats?
    Do you think they're worth the life of
    a boy who's not old enough to have done
    little more than grunt in this world?
BERNARDO: It's too late to argue now.
RABBI: Just stick a knife into his chest
    and take out the heart.
ROSELA: Is that all? And what about the thousand ducats?
BENITO: I have them here, all counted up.
    It's not much for a son,
    but to stop your complaints
    I'll give you three hundred more.
ROSELA: No more than three hundred?
BENITO: I agree, that seems a little unfair
    after all that you have suffered.
ROSELA: Make it five hundred, and let's leave it at that,
    My heart is about to burst again with anger
    the more I think about my poor innocent babe!
JACOB: Please, madam, no more hysterics,
    all the neighbours will hear you,
    and God knows what will happen then!
BERNARDO: If you're not careful,
    you'll lose your husband as well as your son!
ROSELA: I'll try and be quiet then –
    but let's see if you don't cry
    when I show you what's become of my child.
    (*They open a curtain to reveal a heart on a plate and a
    seemingly decapitated child with his head on the table.*)
RABBI: This is a painful sight, I admit;
    but you must think of what's been done

as the only way of saving the children you have left.
One and a half thousand ducats
is no small sum of money.

ROSELA: But think of all the grief these
ducats have caused me!

JACOB: When the grief is over
the ducats will remain;
just close the curtain,
and start the counting.

ROSELA: I don't want to touch them!

BERNARDO: Then don't touch them and don't count them,
but you can say goodbye to the dress
I wanted to buy you!

BENITO: Remember she's only a woman!

BERNARDO: There's no need to remind me, I know only
too well.

RABBI: She'll kick up all manner of fuss.

BERNARDO: And then she'll regret it.

BENITO: Come on, count the money.

BERNARDO: Let the Jews be her providers!

End of Act One.

ACT TWO

Enter the Jews HERNANDO, BENITO, FRANCISCO and QUINTANAR.

HERNANDO: I wish to embrace you a thousand times!
BENITO: Give me as many embraces as you like,
    you'll always be owing me more.
FRANCISCO: I hope I'll be able to fit in a few myself!
    Benito García de las Mesuras,
    you cannot imagine how anxiously
    we have been awaiting your return!
QUINTANAR: I do not expect that I would be happier today
    had even the Messiah finally arrived!
FRANCISCO: Did you strike a deal?
BENITO: A good one.
QUINTANAR: So you were able to
    obtain his magical formula?
BENITO: Yes, I was.
FRANCISCO: Was it tested?
BENITO: It was indeed.
HERNANDO: And did it work?
BENITO: That as well;
    but it didn't have
    quite the desired effect.
QUINTANAR: What went wrong?
BENITO: We were tricked by a clever Frenchman.
HERNANDO: A Frenchman managed to trick you?
BENITO: Sharp though the Rabbi was,
    he was outwitted by this man.
FRANCISCO: How so?
BENITO: Let me explain.
    The sorcery that had to be performed
    required a child's heart
    and one of those wafer things
    that are used by priests
    to feed our enemies in church.
HERNANDO: What strange things one has to do
    to avenge one's people!

BENITO: I wanted to see this for myself,
    and so we went ahead and
    bought a child from a poor nobleman
    who was desperate for the money.
    But he, with the connivance
    of his cunning wife,
    replaced the child with a pig.
FRANCISCO: This is quite extraordinary!
HERNANDO: So the child was able
    to feign his own death?
BENITO: He was his father's son;
    in any case the mother too
    played her part so well
    that we ended up paying the money,
    after which, taking the heart
    and a holy wafer…
FRANCISCO: I can hardly believe this!
BENITO: …that we got from an old woman
    on the promise of a new skirt,
    we carried out the sorcery
    down by a river.
QUINTANAR: And what happened then?
BENITO: All the countless pigs who drank
    from its waters fell violently ill
    and began biting each other
    until all collapsed and died.
    You can imagine for yourselves
    what the impact would have been on
    men and women had the heart been human.
QUINTANAR: It's clear to me there's only one solution:
    to prevent any other Christian
    from taking advantage over us,
    and cheating us so unlawfully,
    we are going to have to steal a child,
    which will be an easy thing to do.
FRANCISCO: But if we do so here,
    wouldn't the loss of a child
    cause too much of a stir?
HERNANDO: Yes, it would.

FRANCISCO: You can be sure that any
    kidnapping in La Guardia
    will leave countless traces.
    This village is so small that
    we'd be caught in no time,
    and we'd lose for certain
    our lives and properties.
BENITO: May I, as a friend who has
    tried to help you out before,
    make a suggestion:
    I shall be happy, if you want me to,
    to go and steal a boy in Toledo,
    and then bring him back here to La Guardia,
    where you'll be able to kill him
    without fear of the consequences.
QUINTANAR: What an excellent idea!
FRANCISCO: It is indeed!
HERNANDO: May the God of Israel look after you.
    When will you go?
BENITO: This very afternoon.
QUINTANAR: I shall come with you.
BENITO: Let's go then.
QUINTANAR: I'm ready.
HERNANDO: Do you need anything?
BENITO: No.
HERNANDO: Well then, goodbye.
    (*Exit QUINTANAR and BENITO.*)
FRANCISCO: I was thinking that…as we've
    decided to kill the Christians
    with the host and the heart,
    and have undertaken to do this
    with our very own hands,
    wouldn't it satisfy us more
    if the child were to die as Christ did,
    and to suffer beforehand
    all the agonies of the Passion.
HERNANDO: To recreate Christ's Passion,
    would be the ultimate vengeance!

FRANCISCO: And the greatest of pleasures!

HERNANDO: I cannot imagine a lovelier day
than the day when I shall witness
someone dying in imitation of Christ.

FRANCISCO: The day will soon come,
we'll make sure of it.

HERNANDO: Great Lord, please help us,
for our pains are growing daily
while we await you!
(*Exit, enter JUANA GUINADERA, PASAMONTES, her
husband, and JUANICO.*)

PASAMONTES: Juana, you must be very careful,
we don't want to lose our Juan!

JUANICO: Oh, mother! Why has everyone stopped here?
Why can't we go nearer the High Altar?

JUANA: Can't you see, dear child,
that so many people have come
to the festival that there's
hardly room for them inside the church?
We shall have to stay where we are,
and watch the procession from here.

JUANICO: From here?

PASAMONTES: Juan, don't be disappointed,
you'll be able to see everything,
we're next to the great west door,
and, when the Virgin comes,
the sun will be shining on her.

JUANICO: If only I could be an angel this evening
and shine like the sun's rays.

PASAMONTES: Whatever for?

JUANICO: Because Mary is so beautiful
that I love looking at her.

JUANA: That's a sweet thing to say!

PASAMONTES: God bless you.

JUANICO: Mother, look, there are
gypsies coming, carrying a drum!

JUANA: You'll have a good view from here.

PASAMONTES: Stay where you are, lad!

(Enter a group of GYPSY WOMAN DANCERS, and a GYPSY MAN; as they dance they form a 'cruzado' – a dance movement involving making a cross and returning to the same position as before.)

JUANICO: How well they're dancing!

JUANA: And how restless you are!

JUANICO: I can't keep still,
    my feet are getting tired!

PASAMONTES: I've never seen such dancing in Toledo.
    Stay close to me, lad,
    there are lots of people from
    outside the town!

JUANICO: I want to get closer!

JUANA: You're fine where you are!

PASAMONTES: Come over here!

JUANA: Lift him up in your arms!

PASAMONTES: You're getting a bit too big
    for that, Juanico.

JUANA: Please hold on to him, I beg you,
    at least until the procession is over!

PASAMONTES: The crowd's not giving me any room!

JUANA: Are they singing?

PASAMONTES: Yes, some courtly 'Villancicos'.

JUANA: I can't understand a word.

PASAMONTES: You'll hear better if you stand here.

(There is singing from inside the church.)

SINGERS:
    'Mother, the falcons
    have flown into the sky
    to welcome the arrival
    of the holy white dove.
    The beautiful falcons
    soar high above the ground,
    and have made the sun envious,
    and anxious to be seen;
    she places on her head
    her finest golden crown,
    to welcome the arrival
    of the holy white dove.'

JUANA: Aren't they singing well!

PASAMONTES: What harmony!

JUANICO: Oh my goodness, mother,
   look at the giants!

JUANA: That boy singer is extraordinary!

PASAMONTES: I take my hat off to him.

JUANICO: Look, father, look, the giants!

JUANA: He's my niece's son.

PASAMONTES: His voice is divine.

JUANA: Can't you keep quiet, Juanico,
   you're getting too excited!

JUANICO: How do the giants eat, mother?

JUANA: They eat sitting down.

JUANICO: What? They never stand at table?

JUANA: No, that would be impossible.
   (*Enter the GIANTS accompanied by a drum; they make a
   full circle and then continue.*)

JUANICO: Do they have their own beds?

JUANA: Yes, they do.

JUANICO: Wherever do they find mattresses
   that are large enough?

JUANA: They give them out in the church.

JUANICO: The smaller giants look really friendly.
   Now that my parents are distracted,
   I think I'm going to run after them!
   (*Exit JUANICO, running after the GIANTS.*)

JUANA: How I always love to hear the singers!

PASAMONTES: They fill one's heart with joy.

JUANA: The Canons are already here!
   The Virgin is getting nearer!

PASAMONTES: The sun seems to be looking for her,
   it's already lighting up the windows!

JUANA: Look how the colours of the glass
   are being brought out by the sun!

PASAMONTES: They're as fresh as the Virgin herself!

JUANA: Oh no, what's happened
   to our darling Juanico?

PASAMONTES: Juan, Juanico, Johny boy! Oh my God!

JUANA: Holy Mary Mother of God,
  my son is lost.
PASAMONTES: It was all my fault!
JUANA: We were both to blame.
PASAMONTES: He must have gone off after the giants
  while I was looking the other way.
JUANA: I knew it wasn't a good idea
  to bring him to this festival.
PASAMONTES: I said that all along,
  but you wouldn't listen.
JUANA: He was crying,
  what else could I have done?
PASAMONTES: But he surely can't be lost.
JUANA: Forgive me, most holy Virgin,
  for I can only look at you now
  with eyes filled with tears!
  Today it is you who are joyful,
  for it is the day of your Assumption,
  and you no longer have a son
  to cause you worries; but you too
  lost yours once in Jerusalem,
  just as I have now in Toledo.
  (*Exit, enter BENITO and QUINTANAR.*)
BENITO: After entering the main door
  he went off with the giants!
QUINTANAR: I thought those were his parents.
BENITO: Those weren't his parents!
QUINTANAR: No?
BENITO: My God, you're more gullible than I thought!
QUINTANAR: Look, there's goldilocks again,
  this time he's following the
  statue of that woman whose name
  we prefer not to mention.
  He's walking towards the choir.
BENITO: What, over there?
QUINTANAR: Do you see where my finger's pointing?
  (*Enter JUANICO.*)
BENITO: My God, he really is pretty!
  If we get him, we'll be made!

JUANICO: I imagine they've gone home,
    and, if that's the case,
    heaven help me, I'll be sure
    to get a beating. Oh please Lord,
    let me have a peaceful night!
QUINTANAR: Speak to him now,
    he's right in front of you.
BENITO: Boy!
JUANICO: Oh my God!
BENITO: Don't be frightened!
JUANICO: Let me through!
QUINTANAR: Don't cry!
BENITO: You're looking for your parents?
    Well, don't worry,
    I know where they are.
    Don't you recognise me?
    I'm your uncle.
JUANICO: You're not my uncle, you don't
    even know I'm called Juan.
BENITO: As you're my brother's son,
    how could I possibly not
    know that Juan's your name?
JUANICO: Someone must have told you!
BENITO: As I'm one of your family
    of course I have been told!
    In any case, my little Juan,
    I have been sent here by your aunt,
    who is of course my wife.
    She wants to see you.
JUANICO: Where is my aunt?
BENITO: She's stayed at home to make you
    a little jacket in silk and gold,
    and a rocking-horse for you to ride.
    What treats we've got for you!
    You'll find large shaded orchards
    laden with apricots and figs,
    melons and quinces, cherries
    and grenadines; muscatel grapes

and sweet baby pears; not to
mention the roses in April
and the carnations in June.
And then there's white honey
like manna, and huge earthenware
jars brimming with aubergines
and aniseed, pumpkins and candy.
And as for the sugar cane –
you can almost see it growing.

JUANICO: Are you allowed to eat all this?

BENITO: Of course.

JUANICO: Are you sure?

BENITO: Why are you so surprised?
And I never even mentioned the
pantry full of pastries and pies,
and cakes dripping with icing.

JUANICO: You're having me on,
has she really sent for me?

BENITO: She even gave me these sweets
and these little boots!

JUANICO: Let me see!
Have they got gold?

BENITO: Yes, just like the jacket
which your aunt has been
working on since yesterday.

JUANICO: These sweets are really good!

BENITO: I was even going to bring some jam,
but it was too heavy to carry
so I left it behind.
But try some of these, instead.

JUANICO: I certainly shall!

BENITO: They're sugared almonds.

JUANICO: Aren't the boots pretty!
Will they fit me?

BENITO: As they've been made for your feet,
what do you think?

JUANICO: Tell me, are there any more
of those almonds in your house?

BENITO: Over forty sacks of them.

JUANICO: And are there birds?

BENITO: Over a thousand,
    kept in gilded cages,
    and with coral and silver plumage.

JUANICO: Will you take me there?

BENITO: Yes, my little one,
    my friend here has a horse,
    the most beautiful one
    you have ever seen.

JUANICO: And where is it?

QUINTANAR: We've left it round the corner,
    all saddled up to take you.

JUANICO: Could you wait for me here?
    I shall be back in a moment.

QUINTANAR: That would be a big mistake
    to let him go.

BENITO: Where are you going to?

JUANICO: To ask permission from my father

BENITO: Your mother has already given it,
    she's happy for you to come with us.

JUANICO: Are you sure?

BENITO: As sure as can be.

JUANICO: Alright, let's go then.

BENITO: That was a good little trick of mine,
    wasn't it, Quintanar?

QUINTANAR: And he's quite a boy!

BENITO: He's wonderful!

QUINTANAR: I've never seen someone so pretty.

BENITO: Can you think of anyone better to imitate
    the death and Passion of Christ?
    (*Exit, enter PASAMONTES and JUANA.*)

JUANA: I don't think I could ever
    suffer more than I am suffering now.

PASAMONTES: You must try and be calmer!

JUANA: I cannot, I love him too much,
    he's everything to me,
    I see the world through his eyes.

Oh my darling son, where are you
hiding your beautiful face?
Who is hiding you from us?

PASAMONTES: Your anguish is understandable; but surely
no harm can happen to him in this temple.

JUANA: But it is here that we lost him,
among these crowds of people.

PASAMONTES: Then what shall we do?

JUANA: Let's go and pray to the Virgin of the Sagrario

PASAMONTES: Her chapel door is open.

(*A curtain is opened revealing the Virgin of the Sagrario
above a railing.*)

JUANA: Oh sovereign Princess!
Oh patroness of Toledo!
Oh Holy Virgin, look upon us!

PASAMONTES: Oh guardian of the human race,
listen to our woes and troubles!

JUANA: Beautiful Queen of the heavens,
who stands serenely above us,
remember the pain when you lost
your Jesus in Jerusalem,
and the happiness three days later
when you found him – now that I too
have felt such pain, please make my son
be found so I can feel your joy as well.
If I have anything worth giving you,
let me offer it as your reward.

PASAMONTES: Holy Virgin, you who are like a tower
rising up above Toledo, please
cast your ever watchful eyes
on every corner of this city,
and let me be your weeping Joseph
as I help you search the son I've lost!

(*Enter a BLIND WOMAN.*)

BLIND WOMAN: You must now say one Hail Mary...

JUANA: Mercy on us!

BLIND WOMAN: ...and one Our Father...

JUANA: This waiting is unbearable!

BLIND WOMAN: And then say prayers to Saint Blas
    and to the Guardian Angel...
JUANA: You wouldn't know, by chance,
    the Prayer of the Lost Child?
BLIND WOMAN: I do indeed, and know that its words
    will console you in your present plight.
    I can recite it by heart.
JUANA: Take this money, and do so then!
BLIND WOMAN: I shall begin.
    Ave Maria gracia plena...
JUANA: Let this relieve my pain.
PASAMONTES: May the Lord help us!
BLIND WOMAN: ...ventris tui, Santa Maria...
JUANA: These words are our hope!
BLIND WOMAN: ...Ora pro nobis...
PASAMONTES: Let them sustain us as we wait.
BLIND WOMAN: On the fourteenth moon of the first month,
    it was the custom of the Hebrews
    to celebrate the feast they called Passover
    in memory of that day when the sea
    parted while their people fled from Egypt.
    And on that feast it was the rule that every
    healthy boy on reaching the age of twelve
    should visit the holy temple in Jerusalem.
JUANA: Already her words are having some effect!
BLIND WOMAN: And the Holy Child became lost because
    he wanted to show himself to the Hebrews,
    and to ask about the mysteries of the faith.
    But Christ was not really lost – he was lost
    only to the Virgin, who did not know
    that he had never left the temple.
PASAMONTES: How wonderfully put!
BLIND WOMAN: The temple was his home, wherein he
                                        could never
    lose himself. But while he was gone from her
    the Virgin was transfixed by a pain greater
    than she had ever known, so great that not even
    all the sorrows on the flight from Egypt could compare.

143

And she whose eyes had never failed her was without them
as she sought to find him among her friends.
And her pain grew with the awareness of her loss.
But after three days she found him in the temple,
where he was talking with the teachers.
And she said to him these words: 'My son,
why have you treated us like this? Your father
and I have died a thousand deaths in looking for you.'
And he replied: 'What made you search? Did you
you not know that I would be in my Father's house.'
They did not understand then what he meant,
but his words were treasured in the Virgin's heart.
And they went back to Nazareth with their
lost Lamb, whose wisdom was greater than that of man.
Most holy Virgin, we entrust to your care
those who suffer what you have suffered,
and let them find in heaven Christ's grace and glory!
Pater noster…

(*Exit the BLIND WOMAN.*)

JUANA: How happy I am to have heard that prayer.

PASAMONTES: I feel the same happiness in my heart too.

JUANA: There is no more that we can do
    to make heaven hear our pleas.

PASAMONTES: Now all is in God's hands,
    we must respect His will.
    Let us mourn no more.

JUANA: How extraordinary, the choir has begun
    to sing in the sacristy. Let's listen.

(*The choir sings from within.*)

            CHOIR:
      'For those who have lost,
      take heart from this:
      You will find in Heaven
      what you now do miss.'

JUANA: Oh my God, if he's already up there,
    that means I'll never see my Juan again!

PASAMONTES: But there is optimism in the song.

JUANA: And what optimism is that?

PASAMONTES: That heaven reveals what this earth hides.
JUANA: There's truth in that.
    Well, Juan, if I have lost you on earth,
    I want to find you in heaven!
    (*Exit, enter BENITO, FRANCISCO, QUINTANAR,*
    HERNANDO and JUANICO.)
HERNANDO: You certainly got a bargain with him!
FRANCISCO: The boy is as good as gold!
HERNANDO: He seems to have been crying less
    ever since you gave him a present.
BENITO: He'll soon get over his grief,
    but, by God, I am shocked to see
    someone put up so meekly
    with so much suffering!
QUINTANAR: What they praised in Christ was his patience.
HERNANDO: Thank God this innocent boy
    has so much of it.
FRANCISCO: I've never seen someone so patient!
HERNANDO: You, Francisco, will have to
    look after the child until
    the eve of the Passover Feast,
    which falls on the fourteenth moon.
FRANCISCO: If you want to entrust me with him,
    I shall be happy to keep him in my house
    until the day chosen by our forefathers
    for Christ to be killed.
BENITO: As you have never had children,
    you can refer to him as your son.
QUINTANAR: Your real intentions in having
    him there will thus be disguised.
    And if anyone should ask any questions,
    just say you have adopted him.
HERNANDO: Shouldn't we also make sure that his name
    is appropriate to an impersonator of Christ?
FRANCISCO: And what is his name?
BENITO: Juan.
HERNANDO: The name is very unsuitable;
    by killing him it will seem
    that we are not killing Christ
    but rather John the Baptist.

QUINTANAR: But we can hardly call him Christ,
  that's such an uncommon name
  that we'd be bound to cause suspicion.
BENITO: Don't be so stupid!
  I wasn't thinking of calling him Christ
  but Cristóbal, which amounts to the same thing.
QUINTANAR: What do you mean the same thing?
BENITO: The name's a derivative of Christ.
QUINTANAR: How so?
BENITO: It comes from the Latin Cristoforus,
  which means 'the man who carries Christ'.
  Which is exactly what a Christian professes to do.
HERNANDO: Benito is absolutely right:
  Juan should be called Cristóbal,
  so that in killing him we should
  be getting rid of Christ and John
  the Baptist all at the same time.
  From now on let's always
  address him by this name and
  make sure he knows it too.
QUINTANAR: But won't this confuse the poor boy?
BENITO: I don't care whether he's confused or not,
  from now on his name is Cristóbal.
FRANCISCO: We have to be strict.
BENITO: Cristóbal, do you hear me?
JUANICO: Sir?
HERNANDO: How extraordinary, he's responded
  already to the name of Cristóbal!
FRANCISCO: He's an innocent little boy;
  he'll respond to anything.
QUINTANAR: No, there must be something in that name.
BENITO: What can it be?
QUINTANAR: I've no idea. Let's call him
  something else and see what happens.
BENITO: Hernando!
HERNANDO: He's not responding!
BENITO: Hernandico!
HERNANDO: He's hiding his face.

FRANCISCO: He really thinks you're calling someone else!

BENITO: Francisco, Alonso, Teodor!
We're not getting any response now.

HERNANDO: Try Cristóbal again.

BENITO: Cristóbal!

JUANICO: Sir? Sir?

HERNANDO: That must be what's he's really called.
You obviously got his name wrong.

BENITO: No, he definitely said his name was Juan;
and that's the name he answered to on the way here.

FRANCISCO: But why are you surprised
by this sudden change?
Surely this is a sign from God,
who has wanted to assure us
that we serve Him greatly
by sacrificing the child.
It is He who has made him
forget his real name,
and take on this new identity.

BENITO: Cristóbal?

JUANICO: Sir?

BENITO: I want you know that from now
onwards your father is Francisco,
your mother's brother, and that you are
going to have to stay in his house.
Cheer up, don't look frightened.

JUANICO: He's my mother's brother?

BENITO: Yes.

JUANICO: But sir, I don't come from here.

BENITO: And where are you from then?

JUANICO: From Toledo.

FRANCISCO: Christ replied like that when he said
that his kingdom was not of this earth.

HERNANDO: I tell you that God is directing
his every word and movement!

JUANICO: Sir, where's my aunt?

FRANCISCO: Let's go Cristóbal,
wait and see all the
presents I've got for you.

147

QUINTANAR: We couldn't have found a better child;
    there's no more need to look further.
    (*Exit QUINTANAR.*)

HERNANDO: If the fourteenth moon is going to come,
    the Passion should start today!

BENITO: Come on, take the Christian away
    and make his sufferings begin.

FRANCISCO: You can count on me.
    A single day won't pass
    without him receiving
    blows or lashes!

HERNANDO: Show some restraint,
    we must try for the moment
    not to excite too greatly
    the Christian mob.

FRANCISCO: Who could possibly restrain his blows
    thinking them to be aimed at Christ?

HERNANDO: Anyone with a sense of danger.

FRANCISCO: If I'm not allowed to treat him badly,
    let him go and stay in someone else's house.

BENITO: You are allowed to do so, but only in moderation,
    so as to stay within the bounds of the law.

HERNANDO: A bit of control will do you no harm,
                              Francisco.

BENITO: And do make sure there's
    enough blood left in him
    for the final day of the Passion.

FRANCISCO: If I manage to see that day
    I'll want my fill of his blood,
    I can tell you!
    (*Exit, enter Queen ISABEL, IÑIGO, DOÑA JUANA, and
    retinue.*)

ISABEL: Welcome back, dear Marquis.
    How is my Ferdinand?

IÑIGO: Showing his usual bravery at Zamora,
    where he fights the Portugese invader.

ISABEL: I would willingly, Marquis, go and join him
    were I not compelled by duty to remain here.
    But in terms of health, how is my lord the King?

IÑIGO: I wish I could say that all was fine;
    but though his general health is good,
    he's having trouble with his eyes.
ISABEL: So the light of the sun is being eclipsed?
IÑIGO: It seems so terribly unfair that
    his eyes should begin to falter now.
ISABEL: That's the way with beautiful eyes;
    they are always the unlucky ones.
    But is anything being done about this?
IÑIGO: A great deal, your Majesty.
ISABEL: But clearly not enough.
    Call for my doctor!
IÑIGO: Your concern for his Majesty's health
    will speed him to recovery –
    a woman's care for the man she loves
    is a virtue capable of miracles.
    The doctor has arrived.
    (*Enter the DOCTOR.*)
DOCTOR: What is your Majesty's command?
ISABEL: My ever vigilant Ferdinand,
    after years of keeping an eye on heresy,
    is causing me worries about his sight.
    You must go immediately to Zamora and see
    what can be done, for he who is the light
    of my eyes needs to be watchful of his own.
    I have a good eye for doctors, and think
    so highly of you that in entrusting his eyes
    to your care, I am entrusting mine as well.
DOCTOR: I shall go and see him, my lady, with an eye for
                               a cure.
    His Majesty has undoubtedly strained his eyes
    through never resting them; but eye problems
    have a thousand causes. Why, only the other day,
    I heard about a woman who went blind from crying.
ISABEL: A woman blinded by her crying?
DOCTOR: Yes, my lady.
ISABEL: What on earth was she crying about?
DOCTOR: A son of hers.

ISABEL: This hardly seems sufficient reason to go blind.
  Did he die?
DOCTOR: No he is not dead, just lost.
ISABEL: I imagine he was a child?
DOCTOR: He was.
ISABEL: Where was he lost?
DOCTOR: Inside the cathedral,
  on the day of the Assumption.
ISABEL: Perhaps her love for her son was such
  that she had eyes only for him,
  and once he was gone,
  she had no more use for them.
DOCTOR: That seems a cruel form of grieving.
ISABEL: I would call it a pious one myself.
  Enough of this, it is time for you to go.
  And I want the Marquis to accompany you.
DOCTOR: Let me kiss your feet.
ISABEL: May God go with you.
IÑIGO: Let me kiss them as well.
ISABEL: My dear Marquis, when you see Fernando
  tell him how sorry I am about what
  has happened. And say I would have
  gone to see him myself had I had not
  convoked the Tribunal of the Inquisition
  for an *Auto da Fe* that I wish ardently to attend.
IÑIGO: I shall tell this to the King,
  whose keen support of the Holy Inquisition
  will make him approve of your decision.
ISABEL: As you can see, our duties are well divided:
  while he defends the kingdom, I defend the faith.
  And now that the Jews are leaving, I am needed
  more than ever to supervise the cleansing of the realm.
IÑIGO: How just and holy are the laws you have passed!
  The world will come to an end sooner than your fame,
  which will be proclaimed from dawn to dawn,
  and earn you both the title of the Catholic Monarchs!
ISABEL: Juana, I would like to do some writing;
  come with me.

IÑIGO: May God protect for many years
    this glorious and enlightened woman!
    (*Exit, enter HERRERA, an officer of the Inquisition, and
    MARÍA, his wife.*)
HERRERA: Are you telling me, María
    that our neighbour is up to no good?
MARÍA: I just don't see why he has to
    treat the child so badly all the time.
    The poor boy is as good as gold,
    obedient and well brought up;
    they say he's been adopted.
HERRERA: Are you crying?
MARÍA: I can't stand seeing someone
    being given a thousand beatings
    for having done nothing.
HERRERA: He must have done something!
MARÍA: If he has, I haven't seen the evidence.
    In the morning the boy gets up
    without asking for anything,
    and then has to wait to lunch-time
    before being given anything to eat.
    Afterwards he's forced to sit in this corner,
    which he cannot leave unless he
    has permission or makes an apology.
    And, on at least a thousand occasions,
    when I've seen him quietly minding
    his business or reading a book,
    his father turns up to accuse him
    of talking or playing, after which
    he's given so many beatings and lashes
    that it's a wonder he's still alive.
HERRERA: And all this for no reason?
    And to an innocent child?
    This is too much! I curse the
    evil man who's doing this to him!
MARÍA: The poor boy's getting weaker by the day!
    All the neighbours will soon be up in arms!
HERRERA: To think I used to be friendly with
    that man, and talk to him often,

until he found out I was
an officer of the Inquisition.
My God, María, we really have
to do something about him!

MARÍA: I can't believe what I'm seeing!

HERRERA: That isn't the child is it?

MARÍA: He's running to me for help!
(*Enter JUANICO, fleeing.*)

JUANICO: Madam, take pity on me,
I put my life in your hands,
and as you're called María,
protect me with your name!

HERRERA: He must be desperate!

MARÍA: I'll defend you, Cristóbal,
I promise you I will.
Sit down on that bench.

JUANICO: I'm trembling all over!

HERRERA: His suffering is painful to watch!

MARÍA: What monster could have
reduced him to this state?
(*Enter FRANCISCO, the boy rushes into hiding.*)

FRANCISCO: Have you seen my little boy?

MARÍA: Cristóbal?

FRANCISCO: Yes. Where is he?

MARÍA: He's not here, that's for sure.

FRANCISCO: I was convinced I saw him.

HERRERA: Be as convinced as you like,
but you're mistaken!
And let me say how appalled I am
by the way you treat him!
I can't see what that little angel
has done to merit all those blows.

FRANCISCO: (I better be on my guard,
that Catholic spy must suspect something;
I always tremble when I see him).
If only you knew what a crafty little
bugger he really is, and the wild
crazy notions that fill his mind;

you know nothing of these
nor of the many other vices
I wish to cure him of –
his snide and impudent remarks,
his perverted desires.
If you knew only half of these
you'd speak to me more kindly.

MARÍA: What could the boy possibly have done to
deserve the sackcloth you gave him yesterday?

FRANCISCO: I can see he has you on his little thumb!
You're the sort who'd believe anything.
You'll be saying next that he's a saint,
or that he's as innocent as the Pascal lamb!
You have no idea of what the boy is like!

MARÍA: What's he done to you now?

FRANCISCO: He almost killed me, that's all;
I believe him to be possessed by a devil.

HERRERA: (He's just repeating something he's heard
from his ancestors; when they called Christ
a Samaritan, they said the same of Him as well).

FRANCISCO: The rod is never used in vain
when a child is being unruly.

MARÍA: But you should never
use it with such force!

FRANCISCO: You say that because you are
a woman and have a tender heart.
Mothers always feel obliged to
give their children presents,
so as to soften the impact
of the fathers' blows.
I know what's good for my boy,
and I'm going to look for him.

MARÍA: May God go with you.

FRANCISCO: Seeing that the two of you
are such pious folk,
you might like to know what
your 'little angel' told
me the other day: "I'll

have this holy temple
pulled to the ground", he said,
"and then in three days
shall build another".
What do you make of that?

HERRERA: Good day to you.

FRANCISCO: You'll have to take it from me
that he's an evil person.

HERRERA: (How harsh the man is!)

FRANCISCO: Do me the big favour of
not allowing him into your house.
(*Exit FRANCISCO.*)

HERRERA: Good riddance to him, that's what I say.
I realise now that he's one of those fake converts
who have held on secretly to the Jewish faith.

MARÍA: How do you know this?

HERRERA: Didn't you notice how he put into
the boy's mouth the very words that
the Jews used as evidence against Christ
when they came to arrest Him?
And don't you remember how the Jews
twisted Christ's meaning, for when He
said that he would pull down the temple
and build another one, he was not
referring to Solomon's Temple,
but to his own body, which was mortal
and capable of suffering, unlike its
replacement, which was the Resurrection?
Don't you see, María, how our neighbour
has used the same false evidence to claim
that his son is possessed by the devil?

MARÍA: I didn't take what he said too seriously.
In any case he seemed a good Christian to me.

HERRERA: I only hope to God that he's cured
of the blindness of his Jewish past!
Now go inside and collect Cristóbal;
take him back to his mother,
who I think would be the best person
to soothe him in his present state.

MARÍA: I'm going.
(*Exit MARÍA.*)
HERRERA: Either I am imagining this,
    or else this neighbour of ours
    really is a heretic in disguise.
    I can only thank the
    King and Queen for bringing in
    the Holy Inquisition to deal with
    matters such as these,
    for the greater glory of Spain.
(*Enter MARÍA and JUANICO.*)
MARÍA: Don't be so upset;
    why are you trembling?
JUANICO: Has he gone yet?
MARÍA: Yes, he's gone.
HERRERA: Cristóbalico, don't cry!
JUANICO: Please don't take me back there,
    that's all I ask.
    Let me stay with you until he's
    calmed down!
HERRERA: What have you done to him?
JUANICO: I must have done something...
HERRERA: Do you know what your father
    does all day at home?
    Have you noticed anything unusual?
JUANICO: I have not seen, Señor Herrera,
    anything that shouldn't be there
    or anyone acting strangely.
HERRERA: I'm glad to hear that!
    Is your father a good Christian?
JUANICO: Only God could answer that one.
    Between the two of them
    there'll be nothing to hide.
HERRERA: Has he often treated you very badly?
JUANICO: I must have deserved it.
HERRERA: Does he attend mass and sermons?
JUANICO: Yes, sir.
HERRERA: Does he take you with him?

JUANICO: Of course he does, and whenever
    the priest refers in his sermons
    to Jesus Christ or to the Virgin Mary,
    he squeezes me tightly and says:
    "I'm going to do the same to you
    so that you shall be reminded of God".

MARÍA: He must be a good man at heart,
    who only acts the way he does
    through shame of his Hebrew ancestry.

HERRERA: But is that good enough reason
    for him to beat the child almost to death?

MARÍA: If the punished child had known
    some evil truth about the father,
    I'm sure he would have said so.

HERRERA: You're beginning to reassure me,
    he's probably a better Christian than I thought.

MARÍA: Let's take the boy home now,
    I wouldn't be surprised if we
    even get an apology for
    how he's been treated.

HERRERA: When he punishes the boy again,
    he mustn't do so quite so harshly.

JUANICO: Please God make me older than my age
    so I can bear all the pains you suffered!

End of Act Two.

ACT THREE

Enter HERNANDO, FRANCISCO, BENITO, PEDRO and QUINTANAR.

HERNANDO: Now that the fourteenth moon is upon us
    and the time has come for the re-enactment
    of Christ's agonies by the boy Cristóbal,
    let us, noble Hebrews, outline in detail
    how we are to perform the final scenes.
FRANCISCO: This dark and lonely cave that we are in,
    which once was used at night by shepherds,
    promises all the secrecy that we require:
    let it represent the holy city that was
    built by Melquisedech in the time of Abraham.
    Let this here be the lower town, and up there
    Sion's Mount, the royal fortress of King David;
    Those shall be the gardens where Christ prayed
    and was buried; that rock can be the temple,
    and the other the Mount of Olives; while this
    brook can be the Kedron, most funereal of streams.
BENITO: You have planned this well! So what are we
                                waiting for?
    Why delay any further our great moment of pleasure?
    To us is now owed the joy of righting the wrong
    done to us by Joseph's son, of pursuing our revenge
    in such a way that we not only take out the heart
    but also take on the parts performed by our ancestors.
    So that our faithful re-enactment can begin at last,
    let's now name the roles, and share them out –
    my own request is that I act Christ's executioner,
    the one who placed the thorns and handed him the cane.
QUINTANAR: I'm already blind with fury and anxious to
                                    begin!
    But hasn't Juan de Ocaña not yet brought the child?
PEDRO: The child's already here, hidden in the darkness.
QUINTANAR: In this gloom I couldn't make him out at all.
    Let's then continue with the casting – you, Hernando,

as the main accountant to the Priory of San Juan,
would be well equipped to take on the role of Pilate.
HERNANDO: I kiss your hands, sir, for offering me this
part,
and suggest in turn you play the high priest Annas.
QUINTANAR: I am greatly honoured by your choice. Now
who'll be Herod?
BENITO: Quintanar could be him as well, and as for
pharisees,
scribes, crowd scenes, and anyone else, we'll all
help out, working out the details as we go along.
Bring on the props then, and let's begin by recreating
that day when Christ entered triumphant in Jerusalem!
PEDRO: Take out the olive branches, throw down your cloaks
Juan de Ocaña is coming, bringing with him the child.
QUINTANAR: Now we have the branches, let's sing the
songs of welcome!
How happy I am to recall those distant times!
(*Enter JUANICO and JUAN DE OCAÑA, while everyone
sings and throws olive branches on the ground.*)
ALL:
'Bring out the palms, bring out the laurels,
and the olive branches two by two:
Blessed be the King of Israel,
who comes in the name of the Lord!
SOLO VOICE:
'Now that he enters into Jerusalem,
triumphant and victorious,
may peace reign in the heavens,
and let there be glory on high!
Who else but you, Christ,
deserves such palms and laurels?
Blessed be the King of Israel,
who comes in the name of the Lord!'
FRANCISCO: That was excellently done!
PEDRO: A superb performance!
BENITO: Back to work everyone!
OCAÑA: Alright, then, Benito,
get the garden ready for the agony scene,
and then see what you can do about a prison cell.

BENITO: Cristóbal!

JUANICO: What do you want me to do sir?

BENITO: I want you to climb up that steep rock,
    and enter the garden that Benito's setting up.
    Then you've got to start praying.

PEDRO: We're completely in the dark!

OCAÑA: I was thinking of lighting a candle.

HERNANDO: A good idea, but remember to shield it with
                                                a cape,
    we don't want the light to be seen from afar –
    there are Christians working out there in the fields.

FRANCISCO: The child is already on his knees in the
                                                garden;
    let's get ready to be his captors.
    Could someone be his disciple Judas?

OCAÑA: I'm bringing out now the thirty coins of silver.

BENITO: And I'll happily act the person who's receiving
                                                them.

    (*Branches have been arranged in a circle to form a grove, in
    the middle of which is the kneeling JUANICO.*)

JUANICO: Dear Lord, make me older in my years
    so I can be a better actor of your Passion.
    Make me reach the age of reason,
    so I can truly know your agony,
    and understand its deeper meaning.
    All your sweet pains I wish to suffer
    for your sake, dear Lord, and though
    they be strange for someone so young as me,
    let me feel them as a man of thirty-three.
    (*An ANGEL appears.*)

ANGEL: Cristóbal, God shall grant what you desire,
    and allow you to feel older than your age,
    This is His way with innocent children
    through whom he wishes to convey His wisdom.
    He has already arranged for the sun to be
    eclipsed at the moment of your death, oh noble
    child whose bravery is worthy of Numancia,
    the Spanish city that fought so hard the Romans.

And in the crucible of the heavens a medal of
your martyrdom is being forged to mark
you out as one of Christ's great men, and for you
to wear as proudly as if it were the Golden Fleece.
(*Exit.*)

FRANCISCO: He has struck the perfect pose;
let's go and seize him now.

QUINTANAR: Take him prisoner!

HERNANDO: You should approach him from that side,
and give him a kiss on the forehead.

BENITO: Hail my beloved master!

JUANICO: Who is it you want?

OCAÑA: How uncanny that he knows his lines so well!
Tell him you're looking for Jesus of Nazareth.

BENITO: I'd rather not, I'm worried now
we'll have a repetition of what
really happened on that day.

PEDRO: You're not beginning to lose heart, are you?
Come on, just throw this rope around his neck
and get on with it!

FRANCISCO: You should be sitting there
to have a better view of the boy.

HERNANDO: Could you carry my seat over there please.

PEDRO: Start flogging him!

BENITO: Wait a moment, before doing so
could you make sure that
the cave door is closed?

QUINTANAR: It's closed, I've checked.

BENITO: That's good, because if the door
was open and the screams were heard,
I wouldn't want some rough Apostle type
rushing in, and do what Peter did,
and cut off half my ear.

HERNANDO: Tell me, what charge do you bring against
this man?

OCAÑA: If he were not a criminal,
we should not have brought him before you.

HERNANDO: Take him away and try him by your own law.

PEDRO: We are not allowed to put any man to death.

HERNANDO: Are you Jesus? Answer me?
   Are you the king of these people?
OCAÑA: This is very faithful to the script!
HERNANDO: I find no just cause for him to die.
QUINTANAR: He hides his evil well.
HERNANDO: You have at Passover a custom
   that I release for you one prisoner.
   Who is it to be this year,
   Barrabas or this man?
PEDRO: That's very noble of you;
   give us Barrabas.
HERNANDO: Did I hear you say Barrabas?
   Well, you can have him.
   Is there anything else you want?
FRANCISCO: Oh Cristóbal! Aren't you going to say
                                        anything?
BENITO: I've never seen anything like this.
   He isn't uttering a word!
QUINTANAR: I'm beginning to doubt he's human!
FRANCISCO: He's going to be sacrificed
   as silently as a lamb!
OCAÑA: Who would have thought this of a child!
PEDRO: His imitation of Christ is extraordinary!
BENITO: It couldn't be better!
HERNANDO: Let's get cracking!
   Throw him in there,
   I want to have him whipped.
BENITO: I'm going inside,
   I've been looking forward to this!
   (*Exit HERNANDO, BENITO and the child.*)
FRANCISCO: Are you sure he'll survive the whipping?
PEDRO: Of course he will, he's a rock at heart.
FRANCISCO: Let's calculate how many
   lashes we're going to give him.
OCAÑA: What about doing this by
   gathering stones and throwing
   every tenth one into a hat?
FRANCISCO: And then work out the number
   of lashes on the basis of how

many stones we've collected?
That seems a good idea.

OCAÑA: I'm going off to get some.

FRANCISCO: You'll find plenty on this wall.

QUINTANAR: He's in for a good beating!

FRANCISCO: They've begun already!
They're really giving it to him!

PEDRO: I hope they don't get too carried away,
we don't want him killed yet, that would really
spoil what we've planned for our final act.

FRANCISCO: He doesn't scream at all!

QUINTANAR: He's a phenomenon!

FRANCISCO: There's nothing he's done so far
that hasn't been faithful to what Christ did.

PEDRO: His tolerance is uncanny!

FRANCISCO: So is his bravery!

QUINTANAR: Especially for someone so young
and so delicate in physique!

FRANCISCO: The number of lashes
he'll receive is growing fast!

PEDRO: Let me see, at this rate he'll...

FRANCISCO: Get at least as many as Christ did.

PEDRO: Over five thousand!

FRANCISCO: It hurts me not hurting him myself.
I'm going in to lend a hand.

QUINTANAR: I'll join you, I'd
like to have a go as well.

PEDRO: Let's all have a crack of the whip!

FRANCISCO: I'm amazed he's still on his feet
after so many wounds!
(*Exit, a curtain opens to reveal the naked child, tied up,
covered in weals, and flanked by two ANGELS.*)

ANGEL: Come on, Cristóbal, keep going!
Let your name keep your spirits up!

JUANICO: Does my soul deserve, dear angel,
a death as sweet as this?
I have now been given more
than five thousand lashes,
and, to tell the truth,

only three of these have really hurt.
Can you tell me why?
ANGEL: They gave you three more lashes
than were given to Christ, and
these were the ones you paid for;
the others were put on God's account.
JUANICO: What? Am I so lucky as to have
received more lashes than Him?
But I would have been happier
still had I been able to feel
every one of those five thousand!
ANGEL: You would have died, brave Cristóbal,
which was not as God intended,
for you must know that when you die
you shall do so just like Christ did.
Which is why you must allow me now
to bathe your wounds in soothing oil.
JUANICO: You are like the Good Samaritan,
curing me with your divine ointment
as I lie wounded by the wayside
beaten up by murderous men.
ANGEL: All these many wounds that cover
your tender body appear to God
like corals and carnations.
But what are these compared
to the pure red roses that
will flow like rubies from your heart?
For your heart, precious Cristóbal,
will be taken out by these cruel men
in vicious emulation of what their
ancestors did to the Holy Lamb,
on whose sweet cross of wood,
you too will meet your end.
JUANICO: Will my heart be used
for any evil purpose?
ANGEL: No, it will not, for God shall
take it for your resurrection.
(*The curtain closes, and there reappears FRANCISCO,*
OCAÑA, QUINTANAR, PEDRO and BENITO.)

FRANCISCO: He's stayed in pretty good shape!
  He'll definitely make it to the cross!
BENITO: There seems to be light coming from his naked
                                                      body!
QUINTANAR: That's the light from the distant candle –
  as soon as its rays touch the pale flesh
  they're reflected back on us.
BENITO: You're right, that explains it.
  Well, now that we've brought up
  the subject of the cross,
  what are we going to do about the wood?
PEDRO: Francisco and somebody else will
  have to go outside to get it.
  They'll probably find the odd beam
  or piece of pine at the mill.
BENITO: They can either buy it, or ask for it,
  the millers are neighbours after all.
FRANCISCO: That's true; I shouldn't think
  they'll make any difficulties.
  I'd better be going then.
QUINTANAR: I'll come with you.
PEDRO: Don't be long!
OCAÑA: There's still plenty of time,
  don't worry; we could always
  slow down the trial scene a bit.
  (*Enter HERNANDO and JUANICO draped in a cloak, a
  rope around his neck, his hands tied, a crown of thorns on his
  head, and a cane in his hand.*)
HERNANDO: Come forward, and don't cry!
JUANICO: Have you seen me crying?
HERNANDO: I was hoping to see proof
  of your sufferings; but
  your soul does not seem human.
  Here is your man, dear sirs!
BENITO: Crucify him! What are you waiting for?
OCAÑA: Crucify him! Why take your time?
PEDRO: Crucify him! What's the delay?
HERNANDO: I find no case against him.

OCAÑA: What more case do you want?
    Why are you being a coward?
    We have a law; and by that
    law he has to die.
HERNANDO: Will someone kindly tell me
    what exactly has been his crime?
OCAÑA: Isn't saying you're the son of God
    sufficient cause for punishment?
HERNANDO: I don't know. If it is, he's yours.
    Take him! He's here. Can't you see?
ALL: Away with him, away with him!
    Crucify him!
HERNANDO: What shall I do?
    How can I crucify your king?
    Can't you see I've got no reason to?
ALL: We have no king but Caesar.
HERNANDO: Come on, see if you can
    make a better case against him.
BENITO: What about the time when he said that
    he would pull down the temple
    and have another one built in three days?
    What about all those devilish tricks
    that were claimed as miracles?
HERNANDO: I'm afraid you'll have to be more precise.
BENITO: I was referring to those acts of sorcery
    by which he turned Jews into Christians,
    bewitched whole villages, and destroyed
    all the holy traditions of the Sabbath.
    His magical powers were such that he
    made loaves of bread come from nowhere,
    and netted thousands of fish all at once.
    And if this doesn't satisfy you, can you tell me
    what law is it that prevents someone being
    executed for unlawfully making himself king?
HERNANDO: Alright then: I'm handing him over.
    I sentence him to death!
PEDRO: You have made a wise decision,
    and one that is in accordance with

the judgement already passed by
our High Priests Anas and Caiphas.
Let us now spill his blood!

HERNANDO: Make him carry the cross on his shoulders!
Take him up to the Calvary, and let him die!

PEDRO: Is he still not crying?

OCAÑA: No.

PEDRO: This is getting beyond a joke!
Don't you realise, boy,
that death's coming to get you,
and that he's not a very nice person –
I shudder at the thought of him!
I wouldn't want to be in your shoes,
I can tell you, what with all the
dreadful suffering in store for you.

HERNANDO: I can hardly wait to dip my hands
in his blood and see him squeal.

BENITO: His blood's reserved for me.

OCAÑA: I hope you keep some for my children.

HERNANDO: Well take him out of here,
so he can get some rest beforehand.

HERNANDO: That's a good idea.

OCAÑA: Are you coming, my boy?

JUANICO: Yes, sir.

OCAÑA: And you're still not crying?
Oh, just take him away!

HERNANDO: Where does he get his nerve from?

OCAÑA: What on earth are you thinking about,
Cristóbalico?

JUANICO: About how lucky I am to be impersonating
Christ.

(*Exit, enter the MILLER and his WIFE, with FRANCISCO
and QUINTANAR.*)

MILLER: I don't know if I've got the sort
of wood you're looking for!

FRANCISCO: What? I can't believe you don't have the
odd beam
or plank lying around! Not even a spare axle or one of

those big timbers you use to turn the mill-stone?
I wish you'd have a good look.

MILLER: I'm telling you there's not a single
piece of spare wood in the whole mill.
Look, I'll ask the wife, if that makes you happier.
Oi there, woman, come over here!

WIFE: Who's that shouting? Is it you who's calling me
woman? Haven't I got a name? Or haven't you
bothered to learn it in all these years?

MILLER: We don't have any spare timbers or other
long pieces of wood, do we?

WIFE: You know very well that our wood was
used up with that silly little bridge of yours.
But what do you want it for? If you tell me
I might be able to think of something.

FRANCISCO: I need it, dear neighbour, for my front door,
which has fallen apart. What with the door's age
and all the rains we've been having recently,
it had rotted way – by the time I noticed this
it was too late to do anything. Well, fortunately
there's this lad who's been staying with us
who understands about carpentry; and he's promised
to repair the door. But as he's leaving today,
I didn't have the time to go to La Guardia;
and in any case, one can't spend too long
with one's front door missing, can one?

WIFE: I've just remembered: there's this piece from an old
cart that's been standing in the courtyard for over a year.
Perhaps that will do.

QUINTANAR: You wouldn't have a spare pole as well?

WIFE: We've got at least two of those.

QUINTANAR: One would be fine.
If you could just sell us this wood,
we'd be very grateful. We're good neighbours,
and we'll do you many favours in return.

MILLER: I refuse to make any profit out of this;
as long as the wood is going to be of use to you,
that's all I care. Shall I bring it over to your house?

FRANCISCO: We don't want to seem ungrateful,
    but Quintanar and I are strong men,
    and can manage on our own.
MILLER: Do you realise I'm strong enough
    to carry single-handed not just the side of a cart,
    but the whole bloody thing, wheels and all?
    Just leave it all to me. Go home, and
    I'll take the wood around later.
FRANCISCO: I wouldn't dream of making you work for us,
    we'll be quite happy to carry it ourselves.
MILLER: Alright then, come on in, and, before you go,
    help yourselves to La Guardia's finest red wine –
    you might need it for the road.
FRANCISCO: May God protect you; we haven't got time
                                   to stop.
MILLER: For God's sake, have a drink!
QUINTANAR: We'll just take the wood,
    we don't want anything else.
MILLER: Well, woman, what do you make of those two?
WIFE: I can't see them ever doing you any favours.
    When there's impurity in the blood, it always
    shows in the end, if you see what I mean.
MILLER: I thought I knew their type.
    Well they'll no longer fool me
    if they say they like bacon.
WIFE: Give them the cart, and the devil as well, for all I care!
    Just let them have what they want, whoever they are!
MILLER: I'll give them their wood –
    so that they can burn themselves with it!
    (*Exit, enter The Use of REASON and UNDERSTANDING.*)
UNDERSTANDING: Tell me first who you are,
    beautiful and gallant lady,
    so glorious and resplendent;
    take me wherever you desire;
    but tell me first your name
    and what you represent.
REASON: I am greatly shocked that you,
    who personify Understanding,

have no idea of who I am:
my name is Reason.

UNDERSTANDING: If you had not come now to talk to me
and reveal your radiant beauty
how could I have known of your existence?
Though reasoning is vital to understanding,
yours is a virtue that only comes with age.
I am merely the understanding that
has been assigned to a young child,
and need more time for my powers to work.
The soul of this child is as great as if
the boy had lived two thousand years;
but until his body grows and his mind matures,
how is he capable of recognising you, dear Reason?
In coming now you have taken me by surprise,
for I did not expect to see so soon
your divine and brilliant light.
Tell me what has brought you here.

REASON: I have been sent by God ahead of time
so that the child in your care
should now enjoy all the powers
of which the human mind is capable.

UNDERSTANDING: And why is this?

REASON: Because if the boy is to gain in death
all the fame and glory ordained by God,
then the use of reason needs to be
advanced in him beyond his years
so that he can fully comprehend
the honour of dying as Christ did.
God wishes you to be with him
at the end so as to ensure that
his understanding of his sufferings
will be that of a man of thirty-three.
Already you have seen how
they have brought him to this cave,
where he has been flogged,
crowned and spat upon.
Already you have seen the blows,

    lashes and fiercesome wounds
    that these bedevilled beings
    have inflicted on his saintly flesh.
    Well now you should know that
    a cross is being built for him
    out of a piece from an old cart,
    and that this cart shall be the
    golden chariot which shall carry
    this new angel into the heavens.

UNDERSTANDING: Reason, now I know why you have come,

    I no longer have to wait to
    understand the world as adults do.
    The boy already has the understanding
    of a thirty-three year old
    to help him bear with saintly patience
    tortures so alien to a little child.
    Already he understands why Isaac
    had to show obedience to his father
    and to accept the necessity of his sacrifice;
    and he has no wish to be reprieved,
    but wants instead to be that lamb who
    took Isaac's place when the sword came down.
    Bravely he steps out now into the fray
    to fight with his cross the forces of hell!

REASON: Move aside, he's coming now.
    (*Enter the Jews, followed by the child carrying the cross on his shoulders.*)

FRANCISCO: Keep moving, and make sure
    his mother doesn't see him!

UNDERSTANDING: Who would have believed anyone
    to be capable of such an execution!

BENITO: Come on, Hernando, help him with the cross!

HERNANDO: If I'm going to be another Simon,
    I'll need to be paid.

QUINTANAR: That seems reasonable to me, Simon.
    I'll pay you myself. How much do you want?

HERNANDO: Thirty ducats.

BENITO: Thirty? You must be joking!

REASON: The barbarians! How could they
    fool around at a time like this?

QUINTANAR: Here, take two ducats, that'll
    be quite sufficient.

PEDRO: Isn't it time we gave the boy a drink?
    What, he doesn't want anything?

FRANCISCO: He's a right little angel! On your knees!

UNDERSTANDING: He is the very image of Christ!

BENITO: My grandfather told me once
    about this woman from Sion
    who used her veil at this point
    to wipe the blood from his face.
    You'd make a good Jewish woman,
    Francisco, let's try out the scene.

FRANCISCO: I'll use a piece of cloth.

BENITO: Good thinking.

FRANCISCO: Has anyone got one?

QUINTANAR: You can borrow this.

BENITO: Take it then and clean his face.

PEDRO: It's folded in three, you'll have to open it.

FRANCISCO: I'm going to put it on him like this.
    (*After placing the cloth he lifts it up to reveal three painted*
    faces of the child.)
    Holy Lord of Israel,
    Look what's happened!
    Three faces have been imprinted in the cloth!

PEDRO: Those are only the marks left by his blood!

FRANCISCO: All three faces are just like his!

BENITO: This is outrageous, the God of the
    Christians has gone too far this time!

REASON: I want to remove the cloth from
    these blaspheming hands!
    Give it to me!

FRANCISCO: Take it.

UNDERSTANDING: Well done.
    (*Exit the Jews hitting the boy.*)
    This cloth is as lovingly
    painted as any head of Christ.

REASON: The blood-red colours are so vivid!

UNDERSTANDING: It could be a portrait of Cupid
created by the divine Apelles.

REASON: A Cupid whose arrows are his thorns,
and whose face still shines despite
being spat upon all by those ugly mouths.

UNDERSTANDING: A Cupid whose blindfold has not
hidden
the radiant beauty of his eyes!

REASON: The divine love that is the Sun
can penetrate through any barrier.

UNDERSTANDING: Only God can be the author of this
work,
and only the sun is worthy to be its frame!
But what is this? What more can those vile men
be doing to our little angel?

REASON: Don't you hear those blows?

UNDERSTANDING: I fear they have begun to
hammer in the nails!

REASON: His pain is unimaginable!

UNDERSTANDING: One day this martyrdom will be
celebrated by the greatest pens!

REASON: Someone will even write a play.

UNDERSTANDING: Look! They are raising the cross.

REASON: How can he still be alive
after all that loss of blood?
(*A curtain opens revealing the child on the cross, all the Jews
below him, and a ladder resting on one side.*)

HERNANDO: We've got the cross nice and sturdy;
I'm sure it won't fall down.

JUANICO: Oh Lord, oh Lord!
Why have you forsaken me?

FRANCISCO: Have you got the tub handy?

HERNANDO: It's over here, Francisco.

FRANCISCO: Do me a favour, Quintanar,
climb up the ladder and
give him a good bleeding.

QUINTANAR: As you wish.

BENITO: The blood is vital for our sorcery.

QUINTANAR: It's all done.

PEDRO: Try and collect as much as you can.

UNDERSTANDING: Have you ever seen such evil?
Reason, let us shed our tears.

REASON: And let the stones and the mountains cry as well.
(*The sound of singing from within.*)

SINGERS:

> 'Oh little Angel on the Cross,
> do not give in now to despair,
> for Christ is watching over you,
> ready to carry you up into the sky.
> Your crystal face for him is like a mirror
> in which he wants to see himself reflected.
> Make sure you show him innocent and white.
> Do not despair, my little flower,
> Christ, who has given you his cross
> will soon be there for you in heaven.'

FRANCISCO: Well, Benito, you know what we need now,
climb up there, and take out the heart,
so we can get this bloody thing over with.

BENITO: I'll go up now, and use as my
lance this sharp little knife.

UNDERSTANDING: Even down to this detail the fate
of our new Abel mirrors that of Christ!
And look how the accursed Cain
has wounded him in the side!

JUANICO: What are you looking for?

BENITO: I'm in a right state!

JUANICO: What are you looking for?

REASON: What an angel!

BENITO: I'm looking for your heart, boy.

JUANICO: You'll find it on the other side.

REASON: How willingly he gives it to him!

UNDERSTANDING: He shows his heart,
and then surrenders it
as if he were in love!

BENITO: I've found it now!

UNDERSTANDING: He has given up his heart to Christ,
   and Christ has given him his own.

BENITO: Pass the salt, would you.

PEDRO: Here it is.

BENITO: I want to preserve it in salt,
   it'll keep better.

UNDERSTANDING: Reason, turn around and look at him
                                            again…

REASON: What?

UNDERSTANDING: …he is breathing his last!

JUANICO: Father, into your hands I commend my spirit!

UNDERSTANDING: He has died!

REASON: What joyful songs shall be sung
   today by the choirs in heaven!

UNDERSTANDING: Today all of Christ's emotions
   will have been felt by him as well!

FRANCISCO: Let's go and bury him outside.

QUINTANAR: We must be careful though.
   We'll have to cover him
   while we remove the nails.
   (*They cover him, and take him away.*)

UNDERSTANDING: They are taking him outside the cave.

REASON: It is fear that prevents them
   from leaving the body here.
   Though they have tried to copy
   every detail of the Passion,
   they refrain from imitating
   the manner of Christ's burial.

UNDERSTANDING: Now they are removing the nails
   and preparing his body for the grave!

REASON: But what extraordinary miracle is this?
   Do you remember how a blindman was cured
   by the blood that spurted from Christ's wounds?
   Well now it seems that the cutting open of the boy
   has brought back the light to his mother's eyes!

UNDERSTANDING: And what fate awaits the killers?

REASON: Death, despair and infamy
   will follow from their crimes.

REASON: Already they are digging into the earth,
    which gives way freely to their spades
    as if from happiness at receiving the child,
    whom they bury wrapped up in the poorest rags.
REASON: And suddenly the world is cast in darkness,
    the beauty of the sun has been eclipsed!
UNDERSTANDING: Oh lucky Spain, how well you have
                              deserved
    so great a martyr and a patriot as this!
    He has brought you more honour still than that
    young hero from Numancia who died with his
    city's keys when he threw himself from the tower…
REASON: May I interrupt you for a moment?
UNDERSTANDING: Sorry?
REASON: The Jews have now come down from the mountain,
    and the skies are opening up so that angels
    can descend and carry the boy's body and soul
    up into heaven, to a great festive welcome.
    (*The child rises up on a cloud.*)
UNDERSTANDING: Oh holy and divine phoenix,
    from your fragrant embers,
    you have flown again into the Sun,
    cloaked in a brilliant plumage.
    May heaven open wide its gates
    to receive you with all the palms
    and laurels that are your due!
REASON: Heaven has gained another angel,
    and Spain another martyr.
    And thus we end our tale…
UNDERSTANDING: …of the Innocent Child of La Guardia.

The End.